SAINT B

The Car

ANDRÉ RAVIER, S.J.

SAINT BRUNO

The Carthusian

Translated by
Bruno Becker, O.S.B.

GRACEWING

First published in French as
Saint Bruno le Chartreux
©1981 Dessain et Tolra , Paris
Second edition, Editions P. Lethielleux, Paris
Published with ecclesiastical approval

First published in English in 1995 by
Ignatius Press

This edition 2017
by
Gracewing
2 Southern Avenue
Leominster
Herefordshire HR6 0QF
United Kingdom

ISBN 978 0 85244 924 0

Original typesetting by Ignatius Press

Cover illustration by
Christopher J.Pelicano

Cover design by Roxanne Mei Lunn

TO THE REVEREND FATHER PRIOR GENERAL
AND TO THE MONKS OF THE GRANDE CHARTREUSE
A TOKEN
OF GRATITUDE AND FRIENDSHIP

"Bruno . . . a man who understood the heart"
Dom Guigo I (*Life of Saint Hugh*)

Contents

Introduction

Some forty years ago the life of Saint Bruno, like that of many holy founders of religious orders, was so intertwined with legends that it did not seem the two could ever be separated. After nine centuries, with reliable records scarce, how is it possible to bring all the edifying anecdotes, recounted generation after generation by hagiographers, into the bright light of history? To touch the inspiring "biography" might risk having the whole construct collapse, leaving nothing but a little dust. Thirty years ago, therefore, the Carthusian Fathers set about submitting to merciless critical examination—I was going to say to a microscope—every event, every date, every statement that would have a bearing on the biography of the founder of the Carthusian Order.

To undertake a task like that required more than courage and daring. To bring it to a conclusion required competence, perseverance, method, and patience. The undertaking succeeded. The results of their long studies are in typewritten and unpublished manuscripts under the general title "To the Sources of Carthusian Life". When we became acquainted with this study, we were astonished: as the critical process proceeded and the legends fell away, the face of Bruno, far from being blurred or mutilated by this severe scrubbing, became more genuine, more lifelike, more spiritual, more attractive. The Bruno of history far surpassed the Bruno of legend. Before our eyes he appeared as the very model of the pure contemplative.[1]

So marvelous a figure should not remain unknown to the Christians of today. The material from this careful study appeared in some pages of the last edition of *The Grande Chartreuse* by a Carthusian,[2] which treat of Saint Bruno, as well as in the important introduction to *Lettres des premiers Chartreux* (Letters of the First Carthusians).[3] There was still need for a more narrative biography, a kind of study of the soul, which would be dedicated, as far as possible, to tracing in Bruno the grace of contemplation, the vocation that, in the Constitution *Umbratilem*, Pius XI called the contemplative life in its original purity. Saint Bruno is the model for the men and women whom God calls to the Carthusian ideal; but all Christians can receive something from Bruno, something for that part of them that yearns to have, besides activity, a private time with God, a little respite, a recovery of energy, a revival of faith and charity.

We hope this sketch will provide that service. Our goal will be reached if, through this biography, people of today will be touched by something of the goodness, peace, and joy that once shone in the soul of Saint Bruno.

[1] Once more we thank the Carthusian Fathers who were willing to publish these studies on the origins of the Carthusian life. Without them this essay would never have been attempted, or, if it had been, it would never have been disentangled from legend.

[2] *La Corrérie de la Grande Chartreuse*, 12th edition, 1976.

[3] *Sources chrétiennes*, no. 88.

Prologue

On a June morning in 1084, about the time of the feast of Saint John the Baptist, a small, serious-looking group of poorly clothed travelers left the Bishop's house in Grenoble,[1] led by young Bishop Hugh. They headed north and took the road to Sappey. After passing the last houses of the town they entered the great forest, cleared the Palaquit Pass, and reached the Porte Pass at an altitude of 4,000 feet. From the pass they descended to the village of Saint-Pierre-de-Chartreuse over a path that today's road follows closely. But, shortly before they reached Saint-Pierre, they turned left into the Valley of Guiers-Mort. This very narrow valley grew narrower little by little until it was enclosed between two steep cliffs. Only the stream and the path found an exit to the west.

The "Gateway", as this valley was called, was the sole entry from the south. A little beyond that, to the right, an oblong valley called the Wilderness of Chartreuse extended north-northeast about three miles. Its lowest point was 2,350 feet above sea level, and the highest was 3,450 feet. It was nearly enclosed on all sides by towering mountains which, at the Grand Som, reached an altitude of 6,000 feet. Except for the gateway of the valley, there was only one other way

[1] This house must have been a modest one. Grenoble had a population of only about 5,000 at that time; besides, Saint Hugh was so serious about poverty that he would not keep even horses to take him around his diocese.

to enter. That was by La Ruchère Pass (4,250 feet) toward the northwest, though the village of La Ruchère itself was accessible only by the dangerous route of the Frou, over two poor paths that were long, difficult, and very risky: one coming from Saint-Laurent of the Wilderness in the west (today called Saint-Laurent-du-Pont), the other from Saint-Pierre-d'Entremont in the north. The latter went through the forest of Eparres, the home of wild animals, and up over the Bovinant Pass to an altitude of 5,000 feet. In this wilderness the travelers boldly summoned up their strength at the gateway of the valley and, since they were looking for the wildest place in this wild place, they climbed to the farthest point toward the north, where the wilderness terminated in a gorge that was enclosed by mountains so high that during most of the year the sun scarcely penetrated it. Amid the fallen rocks the strangely shaped trees still reached for the sky, so that at least their tops might gain the open air, light, and warmth. Then the little band stopped. They had arrived. Bishop Hugh told his companions they should build their huts here and make their dream of a hermitage a reality. Taking leave of his companions, he went back down to Grenoble with his personal escort.

Seven men stayed in the Wilderness: Master Bruno, the former chancellor and canon of the Church of Rheims; Master Landuino from Lucca in Tuscany, a renowned theologian; Stephen of Bourg and Stephen of Dié, both canons of Saint-Ruf; Hugh, "whom they called the chaplain because he was the only one of them who functioned as a priest";[2] and two "laymen", Andrew and Guérin, who were lay brothers. These seven had decided to lead an eremitical life in common, and for some time they had been looking for

[2] Guigo, *Vita S. Hugonis* [Life of St. Hugh], PL 153, 769.

a suitable place to carry out their project. Prompted by the Spirit and knowing surely how well forests in the Dauphiné were suitable for solitude, Bruno came to Hugh, bishop of Grenoble, to ask for shelter and advice. And Hugh, inspired by a wonderful dream, chose the Wilderness of Chartreuse for Bruno and his companions.

Human wisdom would say the selection was foolish. The harsh climate with heavy snowfalls; the poor soil that required so much labor to provide even meager nourishment for its inhabitants; the ruggedness of the terrain that made cultivation difficult in the forest; the inaccessibility of the place during a considerable part of the year, so that there was no hope of obtaining help quickly should there be an emergency or fire or illness. Everything was against establishing any sort of permanent dwelling for human beings in the Wilderness of Chartreuse, and especially in this northern end of it. Several times events demonstrated that these fears were well founded. On Saturday, January 30, 1132, an enormous avalanche fell upon all of the cells except one and killed six hermits and one novice. They were compelled to go back a mile and a half toward the south from the end of the Wilderness, where the Grande Chartreuse is located now.

Bruno was more than fifty years old. Several of his companions, notably Landuino, were no longer young. What secret desire impelled them to brave this solitude, whose severity Guigo, in his *Customs* (*Consuetudines* or *Custumal*) alludes to twice? What discovery, what pearl of great price could make them live "for a long time amid so much snow and such dreadful cold"?[3]

[3] *Consuetudines* XXVIII, 5, L VII, 4. Guigo was the fifth prior of Chartreuse, from 1109 to 1136. The *Consuetudines*, or *Customs*, written between 1121 and 1127, were approved for the first time by Innocent II in 1133.

The mystery of vocation, by which God calls certain people to a purely contemplative life and all-embracing love; the mystery of hidden lives of self-effacement (as it is commonly regarded) with Christ who effaced himself; the mystery of the prayer of Christ in the wilderness during the nights of his public life and at Gethsemane, the prayer of Christ that continues in certain privileged souls at every period in the history of the Church; the mystery of being solitary while remaining present to the world, of silence and the light of the Gospel, simplicity, and the glory of God: this is the mystery we will try to discover in the soul of Bruno.

I

Bruno's Childhood

The six companions called him "Master Bruno". It was not only because he was older or because he had once been their teacher at Rheims, but because they regarded him highly, and respected him. Over them he had a moral power, which radiated constantly from his whole character and could not be explained simply by their past. If they had come to the Wilderness of Chartreuse, if they had joined this bold project, it was because he led them, because they were drawn to follow him on account of the way he had clarified God's call for them and inspired confidence in them. The goodness, the balance, the desire to seek God in absolute and total love that they saw in him captivated. And they were still captivated. He was the one who had formulated the project and carried it forward to its conclusion.

So, who was this man who had such an effect on his companions? Practically nothing is known of his beginnings. Only three facts are certain. He was born at Cologne—so he was a German—and his parents were not without nobility, or at least not without some good reputation in the city. Toward the middle of the sixteenth century, it was said that he belonged to the Hartenfaust family, even that he was descended from the "gens Æmilia", but there seems to be no foundation for that claim. It was based merely on an oral tradition at Cologne. In a document of August 2, 1099, whose authenticity unfortunately is contested, Bruno is said to have refused an important donation from the Count of Sicily and Calabria. "He refused," runs the text, "telling me he had left his father's house and mine, where he had held the first place, for the purpose of being able to serve God with a soul completely unencumbered by the goods of earth." The lack of authenticity in false documents is often camouflaged by some details that are true. Is that the case here?

What is the date of Bruno's birth? We do not know that, but, calculating from the date of his death—which was October 6, 1101—and from the events of his life, there is no great risk of error placing his birth between 1024 and 1031. The year 1030 best agrees with the events that mark his life.

Bruno lived the first years of his childhood in Cologne. No document dating from that period has come down to us.

Cologne! Ancient Colonia Claudia Ara Agrippinensis, which the Romans had founded between the Rhine and the Meuse, had been independent of county organization since the time of Otto the Great, who had placed his own brother Bruno (953–65) upon the archiepiscopal see. He had transferred the administration of justice to him and, to him and to the archbishops who would succeed him, the rights of a count. When Bruno, the future founder of the Carthusians, was born, the name of the archbishop was Peregrinatus. He was the one who crowned Henry III at Aachen in 1028 and thereby acquired for the archbishops of Cologne the right of crowning the emperor. When Bruno lived, there was a historical connection between Cologne and Rheims, which might be of some interest here. He found himself tragically involved in the grave disturbance Archbishop Manassès had stirred up at Rheims by his simoniacal election and by his conduct, while at about the same time the Church of Cologne was experiencing a similar situation. Archbishop Hidulf (1076–78) sided with Emperor Henry IV of Germany against Pope Gregory VII in the struggle of Investitures. Hidulf's successors, Sigewin (1078–89) and Herimann III (1089–99), continued his policy. At least during the period from 1072 to 1082 Bruno surely maintained some communication with his people at Cologne. He would have been aware of what was going on in his hometown. If this conjecture is correct, the great trial of conscience, which prompted him to leave Rheims and join the resistance to Archbishop Manassès, would have come from the two churches that were the most dear to him.

But to return to Bruno's childhood. Archbishop Bruno I, through his talent for organizing, made Cologne not only the first city of Germany but also one of importance in the world. This civic-minded man was also a spiritual man: he promoted the eremitical and the monastic life, built churches, and founded cathedral chapters, so that the city was called "holy Cologne" or "the Rome of Germany". When Bruno, the future Carthusian, was a child, Cologne was still experiencing the intense spiritual life that Archbishop Bruno I had given it. It had no fewer than nine collegiate churches, four abbeys, and nineteen parish churches. At this time, the only schools where children could be introduced to classical studies were in monasteries and churches. To which of those schools was Bruno entrusted? That will never be known with certainty. But, since he was named a canon of the cathedral church of Saint Cunibert, we can with reason deduce that he had had a particular relationship with that church. Was he sent to that school because his family belonged to that parish?

One fact seems beyond any doubt. Even in his first studies Bruno gave evidence of striking intellectual gifts, because while still young (*tenerum alumnum*, as the canons of Rheims will later say) he was sent from Cologne to the famous cathedral school of Rheims. That is where he would live from then on. While he stayed at Paris, Tours, or Chartres, the story was the same. It was Rheims that especially left its mark on him, with the result that, though he was of German origin, people later called him *Gallicus*, the Frenchman.

The schools of Rheims, and especially the cathedral school that Bruno attended, had been renowned for several centuries. Gerbert, who was one day to become Pope Sylvester II, was their rector from 970 to about 990, and they had been enlightened by his talent. In the eleventh century Archbishop Guy of Chastillon gave a new impetus to learning. When Bruno came there to study, the schools of Rheims had attained some prominence, with students coming from Germany, from Italy—in fact, from all over Europe. Among all these young people it was the personality of Bruno that attracted the attention of the teachers.

At that time learning was encyclopedic, and the humanities were said to serve as a preparation for theology. After studying grammar, rhetoric, and logic (the *trivium*), the student applied himself to arithmetic, music, geometry, and astronomy (the *quadrivium*). Only after that came theology, like the crown of all human learning. But if—as it often happened, and a notable example was Gerbert, who excelled in mathematics as well as theology—if one teacher were to go through the whole cycle of studies with the same students, he was allowed a certain freedom in the distribution of the studies. The method of teaching was the *lectio*—a lecture with a commentary from ancient writers who were authorities on the subject. Theology followed the same method, consisting principally of reading the Bible along with the master's commentary, which was based on the Fathers of the Church.

Bruno's studies went like that. Hérimann or Herman was then director of studies (*l'écolâtre*)[1] at Rheims. He did not have the same breadth of talent as Gerbert, but he was known to be a theologian of great merit.

If we can believe the *Eulogies* (*Titres Funèbres*),[2] it was in philosophy and theology that Bruno excelled. But extant letters written by him provide evidence that he was not ignorant of rhetoric. The Chronicle *Magister*,[3] too, asserts that "Bruno . . . was firmly grounded in human letters as well as in divine learning." If we can believe a tradition that seems trustworthy, it is from this period of studies that he wrote a short elegy entitled "On Scorning the World", which would for the first time reveal his gift for reflection. This is written in elegant, balanced, and metrical couplets, in the manner of exercises in poetry that are practiced during the study of the humanities. But just now the thought is of more interest than the form. This elegy, for example:

> The Lord created all mortals in the light, offering the
> supreme joys of heaven according to their merits.

[1] The title of the one responsible for studies—the inspector or director general.

[2] Cf. p. 180 below.

[3] The chronicle *Magister* is a document of the highest importance for the history of the origins of the Carthusian Order. It is the chronicle of the first five priors of Chartreuse. The first four accounts were apparently written by Guigo I, and the one about Guigo was added after his death. The document is earlier than the last quarter of the twelfth century. The chronicle *Magister* was the object of a noteworthy study by the Benedictine Dom Wilmart in the *Mabillon* review, 1926, T. XVI, pp. 77–142. The passage about Saint Bruno was reproduced in *Lettres des Premiers Chartreux*, App. I, vol. I, p. 243.

Blessed is the one who without straying directs his
soul toward those heights and is vigilant to
preserve himself from all evil.
Blessed again is the one who repents after sinning
and often weeps because of his fault.
Alas! People live as though death did not follow life,
as if hell were only an unfounded fable, though
burning embrace.
Mortals, have a care that you live, all of you, in such
a way that you do not have to fear the lake of hell.

Bruno was about twenty years old and still a student of the cathedral school when an event occurred that had to make a profound spiritual impression upon him: Pope Leo IX came to Rheims and held a Council (Leo IX visited Cologne in the same year), arriving at Rheims on September 30, 1049. On October 1 he effected the transfer of the relics of Saint Remi, which Hincmar had caused to be taken to Epernay during the Norman invasions. Now they were returned to the famous abbey. On October 2 Leo IX consecrated the new church of the abbey of Saint Remi. Saint Remi! Bruno's devotion for him is revealed in a letter to Raoul le Verd. When Bruno wrote this letter, he was in Calabria, nearing the end of his life. He had left France and the Chartreuse some ten years earlier. The letter to his friend concludes with these words: "Please send me *The Life of Saint Remi*, because it is impossible to find a copy where we are."[4]

On October 3, as soon as the festivities for Saint Remi were concluded, Leo IX opened the Council. Numerous

[4] This *Vie de saint Remi* is no doubt the one written by Hincmar in 878, three centuries after the death of the saint. Its historical value is small. Cf. *Acta Sanctorum*, vol. I, October, col. 131 to 166.

archbishops, bishops, and abbots participated in it. They were particularly concerned with simony, which was then threatening the Church and urgently needed to be eliminated. Several bishops who were accused of having bought their bishoprics were summoned. The Pope and the Council deposed and excommunicated them. Then disciplinary decisions were made to put an end to that evil. Because he was participating in the ceremonies, Bruno was aware of the measures and decisions that the Council took, the presence of the Pope giving them authority and extraordinary solemnity.

So, at the beginning of his productive life, Bruno was confronted with the great problems of the Church. Profoundly religious and honest, formed by Holy Scripture and the great principles of the Faith, he was drawn to reflect on the situation of the Church, the needed reforms, and the direction his life had to take to reach its fullest worth and integrity. For the moment it seemed the Lord was inclining him to religious studies here at Rheims. There was nothing to indicate he was dreaming of a hermitage at that time. On the contrary, while he was pursuing sacred studies, he was deeply involved in the life of the diocese. The events of the next thirty years would plunge him into an emotional crisis in which what he had seen Leo IX and the Council accomplish would enlighten and direct the choices he would make.

II

Master Bruno

After completing his studies did Bruno spend a short time in Paris? Did he return to Cologne for a while? Did he receive sacred orders? Did he preach? and if so, where? So many uncertainties, and no reliable documents. There is only this indication in one of the *Eulogies*: "He gave many sermons throughout the area" (*Multos faciebat sermones per regiones*). It would not be prudent to draw any conclusions from that, though, because any cleric who had finished his studies with a degree from the school at Rheims could be called to preach to the people.

It would be enlightening for a historian to know when and in what circumstances Bruno was promoted to be a canon of the church of Saint Cunibert of Cologne. Unfortunately, we know only the bare fact, and it is Manassès, the simoniacal Archbishop of Rheims, who gives it to us in the *Apology* that he addressed to Hugh of Dié and the Council of Lyons in February 1080: "This Bruno does not belong to my clergy. He was neither born nor baptized in my diocese. He is a canon of Saint Cunibert at Cologne in the land of the Teutons." We can only guess about the date and circumstances of his promotion. The first hypothesis is to connect it with the reorganization of the collegiate church of Saint Cunibert by Archbishop Herimann II of Cologne. This cathedral church had twenty-four canons. Did Herimann wish to honor Bruno's family and to create a personal link with the church of Cologne for Bruno himself, whose gifts were already evident? According to this conjecture Bruno would have become a canon while still a young man. Or did he have to wait until the excellence of his teaching made him famous? Cologne would have wanted to contribute to the honor being given to one of its sons. That seems most likely. But another theory has often been put forward: that in 1077 or a little later, at the time of the conflict with Manassès, Bruno returned to Cologne. This does not seem likely. In addition to the fact that the documents seem to indicate he and the other canons who had opposed the simoniacal Archbishop were staying at Count Ebal of Roucy's, how would he find shelter in Cologne, where the situation was even worse than at Rheims? In March of 1076, Emperor Henry IV had imposed upon Cologne an intruder named Hidulf, one whom the clergy as well as the people who were faithful to Gregory VII opposed to no avail. Given the present state of research, only this is certain: Bruno was a canon of Saint Cunibert.

If Bruno was born around 1030 (the year suggested above), there is still a problem. What did he do after finishing his studies until he was promoted to the post of director of studies (*l'écolâtre*) for the schools of Rheims? What was his life like? How did he use his time? The answer seems certain. In any city, and most of all at Rheims, such a responsible assignment as *summus didascalus* must have been entrusted to a professor who had demonstrated his abilities. If Bruno spent time at Paris or Cologne, his stays there were brief.

What is more, even before being named director of studies (or at least about the same time), Bruno was called to another dignity. He was promoted to be a canon of the cathedral of Rheims. It was no trifling honor to belong to that illustrious Chapter. "Bruno, a canon of the Church of Rheims, which was second to none in France" (*Bruno, Ecclesiæ Remensis quæ nulli inter Gallicanas secunda est, canonicus*), says the Chronicle *Magister*.

Bruno did not claim this honor for himself. Rheims was then a metropolitan see. Its Chapter, comprised of seventy-two canons, was renowned and powerful. It was directed by the Rule that had been designed for the canons in 816 by the Council of Aachen at the suggestion of Emperor Louis the Pious. It was a moderate rule, midway between the regular life of monks and the freedom of clerics. Canons living under the Rule of Aachen remained secular, keeping their own possessions, having their own house, receiving income. Laws of fasting were precise but not burdensome. Some life in common was required, but it was neither absolute nor strict. In some Chapters this moderation could turn into mediocrity, but this does not seem to have happened at Rheims. Around 980 the Chapter of Rheims was singled out as an example of perfection "in chastity, learning, discipline, in correcting faults, and in performing good works" (*in castitate, scientia, disciplina, in correptione et exhibitione bonorum operum*). At the time of Bruno it deserved that praise. When Archbishop Gervais introduced Canons Regular in the two collegiate churches of his diocese (Saint Timothy in 1064, Saint Denys in 1067), they lived a stricter observance, especially as regards the common life and poverty. The Chapter of the cathedral did not adopt that reform. So, Bruno was a secular canon, never a Canon Regular.

In the course of the centuries the archbishops of Rheims and other benefactors had richly endowed the Chapter of their cathedral. Saint Remi himself (died about 533) had first given the example—he bequeathed to the clergy of his cathedral (the office of canons did not exist then) considerable property, entire villages, churches, as well as estates with peasants attached to them.[1] He meant to foster some common life among his clergy. Other archbishops followed Saint Remi's example. Although the cathedral Chapter possessed many properties, some of them were in distant places, even south of the Loire and as far as Thuringia in Germany. Each bishop committed himself after his installation to respect the Chapter's patrimony. Every year the income from the properties was divided among the canons. So Bruno, like the other members of the Chapter, must have received his share of the wealth. This income augmented his personal fortune, which, it seems, was not negligible. Two of the *Eulogies* from the cathedral of Rheims (52 and 53) relate that, at the time of his departure from Rheims, he had an abundance of resources and was *divitiis potens*.

If we can judge from what we know of the life of the canons of Rheims at the time, this is how Bruno, a canon of Rheims, lived. He lived outside the cathedral cloister, in a house that was his personal property; he received income that allowed him to have a comfortable and easy life; he had servants and could easily receive his friends, since the canons were not required to take all their meals at the common table. Their principal obligation was to participate regularly in the cathedral canons' Office, and we can hardly believe that Bruno would fail to perform this duty faithfully. Did he visit the monks of neighboring abbeys? Saint-Thierry was only a few kilometers from the city, and Saint Remi was just

[1] Flodard, *Historia Remensis Ecclesiæ*, Rheims, 1854 (French translation of the Latin text of the will of Saint Remi).

at the gate. He certainly was acquainted with them and their way of life as his own plan for monastic life matured. When he left Rheims for Sèche-Fontaine he had great admiration and friendship for the black monks of Saint Benedict. He knew, though, that the Lord was not calling him to their way of life.

Outside the time for the canonical Hours, each member of the Chapter was free to organize his life as he pleased. But, if Bruno had been inclined to lengthy contemplation and to a home of solitude at that time, he would not have been able to accomplish the tasks the Archbishop entrusted to him. It was 1056, and he was director of studies for the schools of Rheims.

It would be useful to know the exact date when Herimann resigned his office as director of studies in Rheims, because Bruno succeeded him at once. That resignation apparently took place shortly after Gervais of Château-du-Loir was elevated to the See of Rheims in October of 1055, which, without much danger of error, can be placed at the end of 1055 or the beginning of 1056. Bruno's promotion to the dignity of director of studies would then be during the year 1056.

It was a great honor for Bruno to be selected. Calling one so young to occupy a position so sensitive indicated that Herimann had discovered his exceptional talent for teaching, communication, and even administration. Bruno was only twenty-six or twenty-eight years old. Herimann would not have so resolutely settled upon a man of that age had he not been certain that, in proposing the nomination to Archbishop Gervais, he had the implicit consent of the professors and even of the students of the schools of Rheims. Besides, he, better than anyone else, knew the renown of these schools throughout the whole Christian world.

Rheims was then one of the most celebrated of the intellectual centers of Europe, and he was obliged to maintain its high reputation by the judicious recruitment of its teachers. Bruno had to have already succeeded in the secondary positions that had been entrusted to him before he was placed, regardless of his age, over all the schools of Rheims with the rank of *summus didascalus*.

The choice of Archbishop Gervais was a good one. For about twenty years Bruno had excelled among the teachers of Rheims to the point that one day he was invested by the legate of Pope Gregory VII, Hugh of Dié, with the distinguished title of "teacher of the Church of Rheims" (*Remensis Ecclesiæ magistrum*).[2] His pupils gathered in the cathedral cloister, where the master used to teach. Several of them rose to become dignitaries in the Church. One was Eudes of Châtillon, who, like Bruno, was a canon of Rheims and then entered Cluny, became prior, was later created cardinal-archbishop of Ostia, and finally was chosen pope under the name of Urban II. There were also Rayner, who was to become bishop of Lucca; Robert, bishop of Langres; Lambert, abbot of Pouthières; Maynard, prior of Cormèry; and Peter, abbot of the Canons Regular of Saint-Jean-des-Vignes. Later, in the *Eulogies*, all of these figures acknowledged that the best part of their formation was due to Bruno. Here are some of their testimonials:

> I, Rayner, one of the venerable Bruno's old pupils, wish to offer my prayers to Almighty God that he will give the crown to this faithful man whom he endowed with such grace and piety. I shall preserve his memory in a special way because of my debt to him and my affection for him.[3]

[2] Guibert of Nogent, *De vita sua*, bk. 1, chap. 2.

[3] *Titres Funèbres*, no. 3, PL 152, 556. This Rayner, the bishop of Lucca,

> From the beginning of my religious vocation I, Lambert, abbot of Pouthières, was a pupil of Bruno, that remarkable teacher in the science of learning. I will never forget my good father, to whom I owe my formation.[4]

Peter, abbot of Saint-Jean-des-Vignes at Soissons, said:

> Learning of the death of Bruno, your holy father, the master from whose lips I was taught the holy doctrine, I was saddened, but I also rejoice because he has found rest and now he lives with God, insofar as I can judge from the purity and perfection of his life, which I knew very well.[5]

The testimonial of Maynard, prior of Cormėry, is still more moving in that he was preparing to leave for Calabria when he learned of Bruno's death. He wanted to see Bruno and "open his soul to him". His desire reveals the depth of Bruno's influence ever since those days in Rheims:

> In the year of the Incarnation of our Lord 1102, on the calends of November, I received the scroll, and in it I read that the soul—blessed, I hope—of my dear teacher Bruno had finished his life of a pilgrim on this earth and entered the kingdom of heaven on the wings of his virtues, still persevering in true charity. Certainly I rejoice over the glorious end of such a man. But, since I was planning to come to him in the near future so that I might see him and listen to him, to confide the whole state of my soul to him, and consecrate myself to the Holy Trinity under his direction along with you, I am also perplexed about what to say upon receiving the news of his unexpected death and I have not been able to

---

is not to be confused with Rayner, the archbishop of Reggio, who will be mentioned below. The latter did not study at Rheims while Bruno was director.

[4] *Titre* no. 15, PL 152, 568.

[5] *Titre* no. 79, PL 152, 567.

> restrain my tears. I, Maynard, unworthy prior of numerous monks in this monastery of Corméry, came from the city of Rheims. I followed Master Bruno's courses for several years, and, with the grace of God, I profited from them very much. I thank Master Bruno for my formation, and, because I cannot give him my testimonial in this life, I have now decided the least I can do is give it in behalf of his soul. This is why, along with all who loved him in Christ, I shall cherish his memory as long as I have breath.[6]

To these wonderful testimonials of memory and loyalty, some actions and courtesies of his former students should be added as well, because without any spoken or written word they revealed the profound spiritual influence of Master Bruno. One of these is his nomination to the See of Rheims after the simoniac Archbishop Manassès was deposed and then the call to Rome that Bruno received from Pope Urban II. These important events will be related in their proper place.

Here are some testimonials, selected from the *Eulogies*, given by people who knew Bruno: "He surpassed his teachers and was their master." "Incomparable in philosophy, a light in every branch of learning". "This teacher had strength of heart and speech, so that he surpassed all other masters; all wisdom was found in him; I know what I am saying and all of France with me." "An understanding master, a light and guide on the way that leads to the heights of wisdom". "His instruction gave light to the world." "The honor and the glory of our time". Even taking into account the literary exaggerations that were customary in such testimonials, Bruno is presented as a man who undeniably put his mark upon Christianity during his time. The *Eulogies* stress the value of his doctrine, calling him "teacher of teachers",

[6] *Titre* no. 176, Monastère de Corméry, PL 152, 603.

"source of doctrine", "profound source of philosophy"; of the radiance of his spiritual thought, of his "wisdom", "a pearl of wisdom", "an example for good people", "model of true justice, learning, and philosophy"; and of his knowledge of Holy Scripture, especially the Psalter, calling him "learned in the Psalms and excellent philosopher"; "he had knowledge of the Psalter and, as doctor, he taught many students"; "once the first teacher for the schools of the Church in Rheims, well versed in the Psalter and other branches of learning, he was long a pillar for the whole city."

In addition to three primary and certainly genuine texts—namely, letter to Raoul le Verd, letter to the Community of Chartreuse, and the Profession of Faith (of which we shall speak below), there are two works that have come to us bearing Bruno's name: *Commentary on the Epistles of St. Paul* and *Commentary on the Psalms.*[7] If they too are authentic, as they seem to be, they probably belong to the period of Bruno's life when he was teaching. Both of them, especially the *Commentary on the Psalms*, might have been only notes from a course he gave as professor of theology. Is it too much to suggest that—even if he did not keep these notes and carry them with him when he left Rheims—he at least remembered what he taught by living it in Chartreuse as well as later in Calabria and no doubt never stopped improving his ideas and perfecting them for his own use and the use of his brothers, the hermits?

Is that only a theory? We are certain that, from the time he was a teacher at Rheims, in the eyes of his students Bruno excelled in the knowledge of sacred writings and especially the Psalter. We are no less certain that, both in Chartreuse

[7] *Expositio in omnes psalmos davidicos*, Paris, 1509; *Expositio in omnes epistolas B. Pauli Apostoli*, Paris, 1509, reedited by Josse Badius, Paris, 1524, PL 152 and 153.

and in Calabria, he rejoiced in the fact that his companions were "learned", and he directed his hermits to study the Bible. Toward the end of his life he wrote these admirable words to the brothers at Chartreuse: "I rejoice that, although you do not know how to read, the finger of the all-powerful God engraves love on your heart, and knowledge of his holy law, as well." By their obedience, humility, patience, "chaste love of the Lord", and "genuine charity", they had the wisdom to receive "the sweet and life-giving fruit of the divine Scriptures". Nothing could convey better the extent to which Bruno drew his spirituality and the sanctification of his soul from his understanding of Scripture. No doubt this knowledge was more closely directed toward contemplation in Chartreuse and in Calabria, but could that not be a continuation, a prolongation, and a deepening of his teaching at Rheims?

This conclusion would resolve some of the difficulties that, after eight centuries of agreement, one or another critic[8] has believed it necessary to raise about the genuineness of the two Commentaries. To bring up just one example: it is necessary to take into account the fact that Bruno had meditated, pondered the contents of these two texts over some fifty years, and here and there in his teaching he could have inserted an allusion with a very clear date like the one to Saint Nicholas in the *Commentary on the Psalter*, and that would not be the date of the entire Commentary. Dom Anselm Stoelen had undertaken a critical study of the two Commentaries, but unfortunately his death interrupted the work, and no one, as far as we know, has so far (1981) continued it. At worst—that is to say, even if an inquiry

[8] Professor Arthur Landgraf, later auxiliary bishop of Bamberg, on the *Commentary on Saint Paul*; and the Franciscan Father Damien van den Eynde on the *Commentary on the Psalter*.

came to a conclusion against the genuineness of the two Commentaries—the portrait of the soul as sketched above would not be much affected. Bruno would still be, in the words of one of the *Eulogies*:[9] "a remarkable commentator on the Psalter, and a scholar" (*In Psalterio et coeteris scientiis luculentissimus*).

The *Commentary on the Psalms* is of doubtful interest for the modern reader, and it has in fact been questioned. In the eighteenth century the learned Maurist Dom Rivet said in his *Literary History of France*: "Whoever makes the effort to read this commentary with a modicum of attention will agree that it would be very difficult to find another of this genre that would be more substantial, more illuminating, more concise, and more clear."[10] But in *The Sources of Carthusian Life* he is more reserved: "The Commentary . . . on the Psalms is very dry. Its aridity makes it difficult to read. Besides, it is full of interpretations that are not palatable to our modern taste."[11] Perhaps it is wise to take a position midway between that praise and that reserve. It is true that no contemporary reader should look in the *Commentary on the Psalms* for literary pleasure or even an aid for devotion. But to one who has the determination to overlook this dryness, Bruno's Commentary will stimulate contemplation and love for God. Here are some examples of that:

> "Happy are they who observe his decrees, who seek him with all their heart" (*Beati qui scrutantur testimonia ejus: in toto corde exquirunt eum*). The ones who seek God by giving themselves with all their heart to contemplation are those who, having left all care for the things of this world behind them, aspire to God alone through contemplation, who seek him

[9] *Titre* no. 173. Canons of Nioeil, diocese of La Rochelle, PL 152, 602.
[10] Vol. IX, p. 245.
[11] Vol. I, p. 395n.

> and with all their heart desire only him, who in love delve into the most intimate secrets of his divinity.[12]
>
> "And I will bless your name forever and ever" (*Et benedicam nomini tuo in sæculum et in sæculum sæculi*). I shall praise you in contemplating your name, which is "Lord"; I shall bless you with a blessing that will remain through the centuries; that is to say, I shall praise you by the praise of the contemplative life, which endures in this century and in the century to come, according to the word of the Gospel: "Mary has chosen the better part, and it shall not be taken away from her." The active life, in contrast, endures only in this world.[13]
>
> "In my thoughts, a fire blazed forth" (*In meditatione mea exardescet ignis*). In my meditation, the love that I already had has begun, like a burning flame, to grow more and more.[14]

There is no lack of solemn commentaries like these, which praise the contemplative life and its profound joy. Here are some more:

> Exult in joy, you just, and to achieve it sing to God: that is, praise him in contemplation. Dedicate yourselves to the contemplative life, which consists in devoting yourselves to prayer and meditation on the divine mysteries, leaving behind all that belongs to earth.[15]
>
> "Shout joyfully to God" (*Jubilate Deo*). Praise God with inner spiritual joy, a joy that cannot be explained in speech or in writing: that is, praise him with an intense devotion.[16]

Though some of the writings may date from his time at Chartreuse and at Calabria, Bruno's attachment to the Psalter goes back to Rheims, where, among his students,

[12] Montreuil edition, *In Ps. CXVIII*, p. 528, col. 2.
[13] *In Ps. CXLIV*, p. 560, col. 1.
[14] *In Ps. XXXVIII*, p. 141, col. 2.
[15] *In Ps. LXVII*, p. 270, col. 1.
[16] *In Ps. LXV*, p. 262, col. 2. Also *In Ps. XLVI*, p. 175, col. 1.

he had the reputation of a specialist on the Psalms. Bruno's predilection for the Psalter—if one may believe the prologue to the Commentary—rests on the fact that the Psalter is the book of divine praise par excellence. "The entire Psalter speaks about things above: that is to say, about the praises of God. The book has many things to say, . . . but the praises of God are everywhere. . . . It is with good reason that the Hebrews called this the book of hymns, that is, the book of the praises of God."[17] For Bruno, who had a special gift for praising God, the praise of God is Christ himself: the life, death, and Resurrection of Christ:

> The title of Psalm 54, "For the choirmaster; with stringed instruments; a Maskil of David" (*In finem, in carminibus, intellectus ipsi David*), can be explained this way: This Psalm can be applied to David himself, that is, to Christ persevering in *carminibus*, that is, *in praise*. Christ praises God by his plans, by his words, and by his deeds. He does not stop praising even in his Passion, because it is particularly there that God must be praised *in carminibus*: he perseveres in praise until he reaches eternity; he continues in praise both in prosperity and in adversity, until God leads him to perfect and complete immortality.[18]

The Church has the responsibility and the commission to continue the praise of Christ here on earth, and she accomplishes that mission principally through contemplative souls. Commenting on Psalm 147, *Lauda, Jerusalem, Dominum*, Bruno writes:

> Church, praise the Lord, the Father; praise him as the Lord; praise, and you will truly be *Jerusalem*, that is, at peace; for the Lord this peace is high praise. So, praise the Lord as your

[17] *Ex Prologo*, in Psalmis.
[18] *In Ps. LIV*, p. 208, col. 1.

> God and your Creator; praise, and you will truly be *Zion*, that is, contemplating the things of heaven, and for God this contemplation is praise in which he takes great pleasure. I repeat, praise the Lord, your God.[19]

The heart of this *Commentary on the Psalms* is Christ, the historical Christ, the mystical Christ, the Church. This has long been observed by those who have known Bruno's book. In 1749 Dom Rivet wrote: "Throughout the book, Saint Bruno points to Jesus Christ and his members, Jesus Christ and his Church."[20]

If the critical works now in progress conclude that the *Commentary on the Psalms* is authentic, the outcome would be very interesting, though not essential, for our full understanding of Bruno's soul. If these texts date from his time at Rheims, they indicate that Bruno, the professor of the schools, was already inclined toward contemplation, if not yet toward the contemplative life. If they are to be assigned to the time at Chartreuse or at Calabria, they add to Bruno's two letters a very important note about Christ and his Church. They clearly make the contemplative life part of the Church's very existence and her activity.

Archbishop Gervais died on July 4, 1067, leaving a reputation for virtue. Manassès of Gournay succeeded him under the title of Manassès I. He was consecrated in October of 1068 or 1069. Even though he obtained the See of Rheims through simony and with the complicity of Philip I, the King of France, Manassès I administered his diocese in a manner that gave room for hope of a proper and peaceful administration. But his true character was soon revealed. Twenty-five years later the chronicler Guibert of Nogent wrote: "He

[19] *In Ps. CXLVII* p. 660, col. 1.

[20] *Hist. Litter. de la France*, vol. IX, p. 245.

was a noble man, but he had none of the moderation that should be characteristic of an honorable man; no, after his elevation he adopted the ostentations of kings and the brutality of barbarian princes. . . . He loved weapons, and he neglected his clergy. The following statement is reported about him: 'Rheims would be a good See if one did not have to sing Mass there.' "[21] He was false and two-faced. To satisfy his appetite for riches without losing his episcopal See, he skillfully alternated between wise actions and charitable administration, and the most flagrant pillage. It was in connection with the succession of Hérimar, abbot of the renowned abbey of Saint Remi in December 1071, that difficulties came to light. Manassès at first prevented the monks from giving themselves a new abbot within the time allowed by the Rule; he was constantly looking for a quarrel with them, vexing them, and appropriating many of the rich abbey's possessions. Proof of that comes from the monks, who, during the year 1072, complained to Pope Alexander II against the Archbishop. During the first months of 1073, Alexander II died. In April, Gregory VII succeeded him, and on June 30, 1073, he wrote Manassès a stern letter:

> Beloved brother, if you had regard for your dignity, your obligations, and the holy prophets, if you had the love that behooves the Roman Church, you would surely not allow the prayers and warnings of the Holy See to be repeated so many times with no effect, especially since it was your errors that caused them to be issued. How many times did Our venerable predecessor, how many times did We ourselves beg you not to allow Us to hear so many complaints from so many brothers who were driven to despair! We learn from numerous reports that you are treating this venerable monastery more sternly every day. What a humiliation it is

[21] *De vita sua*, bk. 1, chap. 11, PL 156, 853.

> for Us that the intervention of the apostolic authority has not yet been able to secure peace and tranquillity for those who expected your paternal care. Nevertheless, We wish to attempt once more, with kindness, to bend your obstinacy, beseeching you, in the name of the holy apostles and Our own: if you wish to expect Our fraternal love in the future, repair everything so that We will hear no more complaints on your account. If you disregard both the authority of Saint Peter and—insignificant though it may be—Our friendship, We advise you with regret that you will provoke the severity and the rigor of the Apostolic See.[22]

Through this letter of the Pope there is a glimpse of the cynical game Manassès was playing: there were signs of obedience, promises of submission, and evasion and delay, under the guise of which, Machiavelli-like, he continued his behavior. Leaving Rome for Rheims, the messengers from the monks of Saint Remi carried this letter addressed to Manassès, along with another from Gregory VII addressed to Hugh, abbot of Cluny. Hugh was commissioned by the Pope to deliver the pontifical reprimand to Manassès, and he was ordered to report to Rome how the affair proceeded.

Manassès had foreseen the coup and had prepared for it. Even before the Pope's order reached him, he had placed an abbot of good reputation over the monks of Saint Remi. He was William, then abbot of Saint Arnoul of Metz. In itself the choice was excellent. But, beginning in the summer of 1073, feeling himself powerless to restrain the new demands of Manassès, William asked Gregory VII to accept his resignation. Manassès, he wrote in his letter, was "a ferocious beast with sharp teeth". The Pope temporized. At the begin-

[22] Gregory VII, *Epistolæ*, lib. I. ep. lib. II et lib. III; PL 148, 331 and 332 and pp. 251 and 254, p. 260.

ning of 1074 William renewed his petition.[23] This time he was allowed to take over the rule of his former abbey again. On March 14, Gregory VII ordered Manassès to proceed with the regular election of a new abbot. Henry, then abbot of Humblières, was elected, and he remained in charge until 1095. He was a powerless witness of the sorrowful events that marked the remainder of Manassès' administration.

The Archbishop remained almost quiet until 1076. He even succeeded in regaining the confidence of Gregory VII. He gave official favor to monastic life in his diocese: when the monastery of Moiremont, founded by the canons of Rheims (October 21, 1074), was elevated to an abbey, he made a contribution; he participated in the foundation of the abbey of the canons of Saint-Jean-des-Vignes (1076); and he made donations to various monasteries.

It was during this period that he named Bruno chancellor of his diocese after the death of Odalric. Should this choice be seen as a mark of personal esteem, or was it only a diplomatic gesture? To promote Bruno was to flatter the opinion of the public and especially of the university and to give a pledge of goodwill, so great was the esteem that everyone had for Bruno.

Three documents date this brief period during which Bruno held the office of chancellor. In October 1074, Odalric was still signing documents as chancellor; but a charter of the abbey of Saint Basil, dating from 1076, was signed by Bruno. In April 1078, however, the name of Godfrey replaced Bruno's on the official documents of the archdiocese. So Bruno's resignation can be placed in 1077. The fierce conflict that would ravage the diocese of Rheims for several years began in that year: on one side were Gregory VII,

[23] Cf. *Epistolæ*, lib. I. Ep. Mabillon, *Veterum Analectorum*, I.

his legate in France Hugh of Dié, and several canons of the cathedral; on the other, Archbishop Manassès I, whose lies were at last uncovered.

At the beginning of this unhappy period, Bruno was about fifty years old. Though much history is uncertain, some features of his character stand out, while others remain in shadow.

Bruno, director of studies for Rheims, is seen first of all to be a person oriented toward sacred studies, then as a master and a perfect friend, and finally as a man whose moral authority is felt by everyone.

Even should the two Commentaries (the one on the Epistles of Saint Paul and the one on the Psalms) be found by historical criticism not to be his, Bruno did appear to his contemporaries as an eminent theologian and a specialist in the Psalms. The whole of the *Eulogies* attests that. But his attraction for the sacred sciences (which is clearly more than mere curiosity), notably for Saint Paul's thought and the interpretation of the Psalms, often coincides with his orientation toward the most profound mysteries of salvation. Because of his love for the person of Jesus Christ, he concentrated his attention, the resources of his intelligence, and the effort of his research upon him who was so close and yet so incomprehensible. When the Carthusian Fathers of the twentieth century wanted to express their vocation in a short phrase for an inscription in the Museum of Corrérie, they borrowed this text from the Epistle to the Colossians: "Your life is hidden with Christ in God" (*Vita vestra abscondita est cum Christo in Deo*). The simple facts of history are enough: Bruno had decided to consecrate his life to the study and teaching of the Faith, and the things of God had captivated his heart and brought satisfaction to his life.

Not only a renowned scholar but also a master, in the fully

human sense that Saint Augustine gives the word, Bruno was an excellent teacher. His learning was not only scholarship: Bruno exercised the spiritual influence that the *Eulogies* speak of only because his teaching had been inspired by a profound interest in man and had deeply touched the religious beliefs and the essential restlessness of his hearers. He made his pupils into disciples, often into friends. In the *Eulogies* regret is often mingled with warm emotion, beyond literary convention and catharsis. Bruno aroused more than admiration because he offered and enkindled friendship. The later years of his life will prove him better still, because the three in Adam's little garden were friends that day they determined to turn their life completely over to God, three friends bound together by their desire for the things of eternity.

At the end of this long first part of his life Bruno appeared a man of undisputed moral honor and distinction. It was by no intrigue that the holy Bishop Gervais and Master Herimann had agreed to confer the charge of director of studies for Rheims upon a young man who was not yet thirty years old. During the twenty years that he held this office, Bruno must have acquired a reputation for undisputed integrity and authority, because Manassès I in his anxiety chose him to be chancellor for the purpose of convincing Gregory VII of his good intentions. Wasn't Bruno's early resignation from the office of chancellor another proof of his integrity? Bruno was a just man, in the biblical sense of the word. Like William, the abbot of Saint Arnoul, he quickly took the measure of the Archbishop and his corruption, and it seemed he could have peace only by removing himself from every risk of compromise and recovering his freedom to judge and, if necessary, to oppose.

In every society, but especially in a corrupt one, such devotion for the word of God, such love of noble friendship, such integrity destine a person to be, in a real sense, solitary. One who is guileless is always in some way alone. Bruno was already a "master", not only in the sense that he mastered his teaching and deeply influenced his pupils but even more in the sense that he directed events as well as people. He was above them; he was greater than they; he looked upon them from his higher vantage point; he saw and judged them. The power of his personality is demonstrated in the momentous events that are about to buffet the Church of Rheims.

III

Bruno Confronts Archbishop Manassès

In 1075 the spiritual power of the Pope and the temporal power of the princes began the long struggle that is known in history as the struggle of investitures.

Since his election in March of 1074, Gregory VII had energetically continued the Church reform that his predecessor had initiated. In 1075 he renewed Alexander's decrees and strengthened them, condemning the investiture of bishops by temporal princes. In France the legate commissioned to enforce the papal decree was an inflexible, merciless man called Hugh of Dié. His task was thankless, but he undertook it vigorously. It has been written that he was "the most despised man of the eleventh century", and he was called "the Church's hatchet man" in France. At the Pope's command Hugh had to call a series of regional councils that bishops who were suspected of simony were required to attend, and those who were found guilty were dismissed from their office and replaced with trustworthy bishops. The first of those councils was held in 1075 at Anse, near Lyons. The battle was begun in the name of the Pope against the dreadful scourge of simony, and everyone took a stand on the papal reform.

The Council of Clermont was held during the summer of

1076. The Provost of the Chapter of Rheims, who like his Archbishop was called Manassès, came of his own accord to Hugh of Dié and admitted that he had bought his office at the beginning of 1075 after the death of the provost Odalric. He humbly asked to be forgiven.

It was on the occasion of that meeting, no doubt, that the Provost Manassès acquainted Hugh of Dié with the extraordinary situation in which Archbishop Manassès had, through corruption and violence, involved the diocese of Rheims: the depreciation of possessions of the Church, arbitrary exactions from clergy and monks, traffic in offices and benefices, excommunication threatened against any who opposed him. The higher authority had to intervene.

Why? Was it because of that complaint and to circumvent the Archbishop's anger? During the last months of 1076 several important individuals went into voluntary exile from Rheims, risking the loss of their positions and their possessions. Ebal,[1] count of Roucy-sur-l'Aisne, offered them a place of refuge. The names of some of these complainants are known: there were the Provost Manassès, Bruno, Raoul le Verd, and Fulco le Borgne. And these were surely not the only ones.

The tension between the Archbishop and the exiles soon reached a critical point. When Gregory VII was informed of the situation, he decided to intervene, which he did with prudence and moderation. On March 25, 1077, he directed the Bishop of Paris to examine the dossier of several who had, apparently, been unjustly threatened with excommunication by Manassès, still regarding him as the lawful shepherd of the Church of Rheims. On May 12 of the same year he again chose him to sit beside Hugh, the abbot of Cluny,

[1] Or Hebal, or Eblo.

at the head of the Council that was about to take place at Langres.

All at once the situation was completely reversed. The plans for Langres were canceled. The Council would be held at Autun on September 10, 1077. Instead of presiding there as judge, Bishop Manassès would be summoned and accused. He refused to appear. But those in exile at Roucy, including the Provost Manassès and Bruno, came, and they accused their Archbishop of having obtained the See of Rheims by simony and, despite the formal prohibition of the Pope, of having consecrated the Bishop of Senlis, who had received his See through lay investiture at the hands of the King of France. Bishop Manassès was suspended from his position by the Fathers of the Council, "because, though summoned to the Council to give an account of himself, he did not come" (*quid vocatus ad Concilium ut se purgaret, non venit*).

Manassès responded immediately with severe reprisals against the clerics of Rheims who had gone to Autun. "As the canons of Rheims were returning after making their accusations against him at the Council," writes Hugh of Flavigny in his *Chronicle*, "the Archbishop ambushed them, sacked their houses, sold what they had to live on, and confiscated their possessions."

Regardless of the suspension[2] threatened by the fathers of the Council of Autun, the dispute between Bishop Manassès and the canons was not resolved. What followed indicates that the Chapter of Rheims and the legate, Hugh of Dié, must have felt it urgent to inform Gregory VII. If Marlow's *History of the Church of Rheims* can be believed, the Chap-

[2] A canonical penalty by which a member of the clergy is deprived of his office and his benefice.

ter would have sent Bruno himself (and perhaps Manassès) to Rome so they could tell the Pope personally about the excesses of the Archbishop. Be that as it may, an account by Hugh of Dié relates (some authors say it was through two letters) the part played by the Provost and by Bruno in the resistance to the Bishop. The delegate to Gregory VII wrote:

> To Your Holiness we recommend our friend in Christ, Manassès, who resigned his office of provost of the Church of Rheims during the Council of Clermont. Though he had obtained his position unlawfully, he is a sincere defender of the Catholic Faith. We also recommend Bruno, a teacher with integrity in the Church of Rheims. Both of them deserve to be confirmed for divine service by your authority, because they have been judged worthy of suffering persecution for the name of Jesus. Please use them as your counsellors and cooperators for the cause of God in France.

This is an authentic and important testimonial to the high regard that the legate and everyone else at Rheims (except the simoniac Archbishop) had for Bruno. For Hugh of Dié to bestow so formal an encomium upon someone, saying, "His life is irreproachable" or calling him "master of all integrity in the Church of Rheims", there must have been no shadow on his conduct. Bruno's faith, virtue, and honor were beyond suspicion. He stood above this troubled period for the Church of Rheims like one without guile, who had not compromised at all.

As a matter of fact, Gregory VII did not confirm the judgment of the Council of Autun immediately. He soon wrote that the Roman Church was accustomed to act with "a measure of discretion rather than the rigor of law". The Pope recognized his legate's tendency to be severe. Had he not perhaps judged too quickly, extinguishing the wick instead of encouraging it to flame again? He decided to examine the case of Manassès himself, as well as the six other bishops who had been condemned by Hugh of Dié. To do that he called them to Rome and invited them to explain. Count Ebal of Roucy, and Ponce, one of the canons of Rheims, came with them to tell Gregory VII just what had happened at Rheims. At Rome the discussion was difficult. The principal argument that Manassès dared to propose in his own defense was that to condemn him would be to risk creating a schism within the kingdom![3] Finally Manassès flared up at his accusers. Upon an oath "on the body of Saint Peter", he obtained pardon from Gregory VII. On March 9, 1078, Gregory VII addressed the following letter to the legate:

> Because it is the custom of the Roman Church, at the head of which God has placed Us in spite Our unworthiness, to tolerate certain actions and to let some pass in silence, We have decided to use moderation rather than demand the strictness of the law, and We have very carefully reexamined the cases of the bishops of France who were suspended or condemned by our legate, Hugh of Dié. Although Manassès, the Archbishop of Rheims, has been accused on several counts, and although he refused to appear at the Council to which Hugh of Dié had summoned him, it seems to Us that the sentence against him was not in conformity with the compassion and gentleness customary in the Roman Church. For this reason We restored him to the duties of his office after he took this oath on the body of Saint Peter: "I, Manassès, declare that it was not out of pride that I did not appear at the Council of Autun, to which the Bishop of Dié had summoned me. If I were called by a messenger or a letter from the Holy See, I would not use any pretext or deceit to escape. I would come and loyally submit to the decision and judgment of the

[3] *Epistolæ* lib. VII, ep. XII, PL 148, 556.

Church. If it pleases Pope Gregory or his successor that I give an account before his legate, I shall obey with the same humility. I shall not use the treasures, the resources, or the possessions of the Church of Rheims, which are entrusted to my care, except for the honor of that church, and I shall not dispose of them in any way that I could be accused of failing in justice." So, Manassès was enfolded in a judgment of leniency and mercy, which closed the inquiry and the case of the bishops.[4]

This gentleness was not what the legate, Hugh of Dié, wanted from the Pope. Would it not destroy his authority? He wrote to the Pope with some bitterness to let him know of his disagreement:

> May Your Holiness grant that no longer will anyone insult us and dishonor us. Those that we suspended, deposed, or even condemned, who were guilty of simony or anything else, freely have recourse to Rome, and there, where they should meet with strict justice, they find the mercy they desire. Those who previously did not dare to sin even in trifling things, begin to indulge in more profitable dealings, tyrannizing over the churches they are in charge of. Believe me, most holy Father, Your Holiness' useless servant.[5]

No doubt the legate's complaint went beyond the case of the Archbishop of Rheims, but it did include him. Returning to his diocese, Manassès played the penitent to extend and consolidate his victory. He attempted to be reconciled with the Provost, with Bruno, and with the other canons who had taken refuge with Count Ebal and, in good time and in proper form, to obtain a papal condemnation against the Count. To free his hands for further intrigues, he even

[4] *Epistolæ*, lib. V. ep. XVII, PL 148, 502.

[5] *Chronicon*, lib. II, PL 154, 287D.

asked the Pope to make him subject no longer to the jurisdiction of Hugh of Dié any longer but only to the authority of the Pope or legates who come from Rome. Then with shameless wheedling he wrote at length to Gregory VII. He repeatedly proclaimed his fidelity and homage; he accused, he argued, he invoked the privileges granted to his predecessors; and finally he came to the exiles and their protector:

> As regards Count Ebal, who attempted to accuse me in your presence, appealed to you, and affirmed his fidelity to you with hypocritical words, you were able to recognize which side was showing you sincerity and fidelity: mine, where I am prepared to obey God and you in everything, or the side of the Count of Ebal, who in your presence attacked the Church of Saint Peter and in our presence persecutes the Church of Rheims through the Provost Manassès and his partisans, who gathered at his chateau. This Manassès has received the assurance of forgiveness, which you ordered us to grant him if he returned to the Church, his mother; but, paralyzed in the knowledge of his sins, he chooses neither to return to us nor to yield to the peace of the Church. On the contrary, he does not cease, nor do his followers, to revile my church and myself by derogatory language, since he may not inflict physical blows. Further, without speaking of Count Ebal, who, I trust, will not escape your just and apostolic sentence, I urgently beseech your Holiness to order Manassès to return home and attack his church no longer; or better, frighten him and his supporters and his cooperators with a stern, apostolic sentence. Be so kind as to write to those who have received them and tell them to give them asylum against the rights of the Church no longer under pain of similar sentence.[6]

It was a deceitful tactic. The phrase "without speaking of Count Ebal" insinuates that the sentence of condemna-

[6] *Epistola Manassæ*, PL 148, 743.

tion has passed from himself. Putting that first, in the place of Manassès, who was not without reproach; saying nothing about Bruno, whom, the Archbishop well knew, the Pope considered a virtuous and honorable man—all that was clever, too clever. The Pope did not permit himself to be taken by surprise again. He outmaneuvered every trap. On August 22, 1078, he sent a reply to Manassès' letter. In his excellent reply the Pontiff again attempted to avoid an open break with the Archbishop and to design an honorable withdrawal for him if he should agree to be sincere and trustworthy. He reassured him of his loyalty and guaranteed him his rights as bishop and metropolitan. But Manassès will give up every exemption: he will not place himself above the law, and he will recognize the authority of the papal legates even if they do not come from Rome, specifically the authority of Hugh of Dié with whom, in an effort to avoid any excessive strictness, he associated the Abbot of Cluny, who was known for his moderate judgments. The Provost Manassès too will be subjected to a just and precise investigation by the two legates: "Regarding the Provost Manassès who, you say, never ceases to annoy you by his words since he cannot do it by his acts, and against whom you have made any other accusations you please, We are sending you Our instructions for Our dear brothers the Bishop of Dié and the Abbot of Cluny, so that they will try to conduct a diligent inquiry into these affairs, to examine them carefully, and to judge them in all truth and justice in conformity with canon law."[7]

For the Pope, these were not idle words. On that very day he sent his instructions to Hugh of Dié and Hugh of Cluny. They were measured words. Gregory VII's wisdom

[7] *Epistolæ*, lib. VI, ep. II, PL 148, 510.

and his perfect knowledge of each of his collaborators shine through them. He directed the legates to "strive to reconcile the provost Manassès, whom the Archbishop complained of, the one who had fled to Count Ebal and, aided by him, has not ceased to disturb the Archbishop and his church. He should desist from disturbing the church and persecuting the Bishop. If he is stubborn and does not wish to obey, do with him what seems right to you." To the Provost these instructions seemed to be harsh, and they were. They reveal the seriousness of the conflict that set the Archbishop and the exiled canons against each another. But the Pope added a little clause that showed that he was well informed about the matter and wondered whether the Provost's resistance might not be justified: "Unless you find out that he has just cause for what he is doing". Everything should be done in accordance with law and justice. In charity, the legates will place all their energy at the service of law and justice. In this painful conflict charity must prevail.

> Regarding the other demands of the Archbishop, assist him as is proper, if he obeys you, and with the authority of the apostles defend the church which has been placed in his care. As regards himself, We have been informed by the letters you have written to Us that he is seeking delays and deceit. We have told him by letter exactly what We are writing to you today. My dear brothers, act with strength and wisdom, and do everything with charity. May the oppressed find you prudent defenders, and may their oppressors see your love of justice. May the all-powerful God pour his Spirit into your hearts!"[8]

We do not know for sure what happened at the end of 1078 and during the first months of 1079. The fact is that,

[8] *Epistolæ*, lib. VI, ep. III, PL 148, 512.

at midsummer of that year, the legate Hugh of Dié, in agreement with the Abbot of Cluny, judged it expedient to convoke a Council at Trent and summon Archbishop Manassès to it. He came, along with an escort of numerous supporters, intending that their show of numbers would surely bring pressure upon the Council. Did he do this to prevent the Council from deliberating or making free judgments? At the last moment the legate canceled the Council.

Gregory VII decided to intervene and subject the Archbishop's conduct to a new scrutiny. He wrote this order to Hugh of Dié:

> Since you were unable to convoke a Council in the place that was planned, We judge it advisable now that you find a suitable location to hold a synod and carefully examine the case of the Archbishop of Rheims. If trustworthy accusers and witnesses are found who can prove canonically the charges against him, We desire that you carry out without delay the sentence that justice will determine. On the other hand, if such witnesses cannot be found, now that this Archbishop's reputation for scandal has spread not only throughout France but also almost all of Italy, let him bring, if he can, six bishops of unblemished character. If they find him innocent, he will be exonerated and permitted to live at peace in his church with his prerogatives.[9]

To put this case in perspective, the conflict in which the provost Manassès, Bruno, and the canons of Rheims were involved was not an internal dispute in a single diocese, a mere "sacristy argument". The importance of Rheims in France and the pompous excesses of the Archbishop took the affair beyond the diocese of Rheims. The scandal touched all of France and most of Italy. For that reason Gregory VII

[9] *Epistolæ*, PL 148, 695.

imposed this unusual procedure upon his legates. If the witnesses for the prosecution failed to make the accusation clear and undeniable, the Archbishop would not for that reason be found innocent; it would be for him to prove positively that his conduct and his intentions were honorable. Six bishops "of unblemished character" must personally attest to the morality of his conduct and his fitness to remain at the head of the Church of Rheims. This policy was a strong challenge to Manassès and his intrigues.

Following the Pope's orders, Hugh of Dié convoked a new council. Lyons was chosen to be the place for it. The date was set for the first days of February 1080. Manassès again appealed to the Pope over the head of the legate, invoking an ancient privilege of the Church of Rheims according to which the Archbishop was responsible only to the Holy See. Gregory VII responded on January 5, 1080, refusing him the right to challenge the jurisdiction of his legate, Hugh of Dié, who would be assisted by the Bishop of Albano, Cardinal Peter Ignée, and Hugh of Cluny. Gregory wrote:

> We are astonished that so wise a man as you finds so many excuses to remain isolated and hold on to your church in the face of such disgraceful accusations and allow public opinion to judge you, when you should be interested in removing suspicions like these and freeing your church from them. If you do not go to the Council of Lyons, if you do not obey the Roman Church, which has put up with you for a long time, We shall in no way change the decision of the Bishop of Dié; rather, We shall confirm it by Our apostolic authority.[10]

The threat was clear. Giving up his hope to deceive Gregory VII, Manassès tried to bribe Hugh, the abbot of

[10] *Epistolæ* XII, PL 148, 556.

Cluny. He sent secret messengers to offer him 300 ounces of pure gold as well as gifts for his friends. He promised still greater gifts if he would be permitted to vindicate himself. The Abbot of Cluny was unmoved by these offers.

At the beginning of February 1080, the Council assembled at Lyons as planned. Regardless of the Pope's threat, Manassès did not come in person. He sent an *Apology*[11] in which, without refuting the accusations brought against him, he attacked the procedures and the conditions imposed upon him. He took up an argument that he had already used with Gregory VII: going to Lyons would place him in real danger; how could he find six bishops to testify on his behalf? how could he find them in the twenty days that remained? and who would be the judge of the character of the six bishops? We should cite two passages of this prideful *Apology* that refer to Bruno:

> You tell me first to come to the Council and respond to my accusers, Provost Manassès and his companions. But I say to you that I have come to an agreement with Manassès with regard to all of his followers except for two, one of whom is Bruno. But this Bruno does not belong to my church. He was not born there, nor was he baptized there. He is a canon of Saint Cunibert in Cologne, in the land of the Teutons. Having absolutely no knowledge of his life and background, I do not value his presence here very much. Besides, I have bestowed many benefits upon him since he came to live here, and in return I have received from him only malicious and undeserved treatment. As regards the other one, Ponce, he lied in my presence before the Roman Council, and that is why I do not wish nor should I be required to respond to either one of them in an ecclesiastical court.

[11] *L'Apologie de Manassès* was published for the first time by Mabillon. *Musæum ital.* vol. I, pt. II, pp. 117–22 circiter.

A little farther on, the Archbishop returns to his topic:

> As I have said, I would not accept any accusation made by the provost Manassès and his companions—unless, at the Council, they return to their error—because they have been reconciled with me, except for Bruno and Ponce, as I said, and to them I do not wish nor should I be required to respond for the reason I have already stated. If some of them with whom I have made peace through the mediation of the provost Manassès should come to the Council in contempt of that peace and should wish to say something against me, their testimony would not be admissible because, at the time of the agreement, they were not familiar to me either as friends or canons, and so they could not offer testimony about my life.

These texts are very important. They prove that the provost Manassès had yielded to the pressure and the offers of the Archbishop, and that Bruno and Ponce had not agreed to follow him and capitulate. If by itself their refusal may be ambiguous (was it from obstinacy, or was it from clarity of vision and disinterestedness?), the events to follow will remove the ambiguity and justify the position taken by Bruno and Ponce. Another item equally important is that Bruno did not appear in the foreground until after the Provost's reconciliation with the Archbishop; until then it was the Provost who was at the head of the group of exiles, so that, having won him back to his side, the Archbishop considered that the resistance ("his accusers") no longer existed. In this diatribe the Archbishop apologized to Bruno without wanting to, even before he actually offered an apology. This shows us one of Bruno's attributes that we will find throughout the course of his life: an admirable strength of character to pursue, to the end and come what may, whatever he believed to be the will of God for him, and no difficulty, no threat, no promise, no desertion could succeed in deflecting him from something he had undertaken, once he judged in conscience that the undertaking was the will of God.

The *Apology* could not save Archbishop Manassès. The Fathers of the Council deposed him from the episcopacy. In March of 1080, Hugh of Dié went to Rome to tell Gregory VII what had happened. On April 17, 1080, the Pope wrote to Manassès to let him know that during the spring synod at Rome he had confirmed the verdict of Lyons. Even in this extremity, however, the Pope, "moved by mercy that is, I might say, excessive" (*nimia, ut ita dixerim, misericordia ductus*), offered him a chance to repair his reputation, if not his situation. Manassès could ask "by Saint Michael" for six bishops in whom the Pope had confidence (those of Soissons, Laon, Cambrai, Châlons-sur-Marne, and two others) to testify in his behalf. To this generous gesture Gregory VII attached only a few conditions that were very reasonable. The Archbishop will restore to them all the possessions he had taken "from Manassès, from Bruno, and from the other canons who, in speaking [against him], seemed to have no other purpose than to secure justice"; he will not oppose the return of those who have suffered exile so long for the sake of justice, and he will permit them to serve God in the Church of Rheims with security; and before the feast of the Ascension the following year he will vacate the Church of Rheims and withdraw willingly to Cluny or to Chaise-Dieu, there to live in seclusion at his own expense with one cleric and two laymen after swearing before the legate that he will take nothing that belongs to Rheims except what is necessary for his livelihood and that of his companions. If he refuses to obey, Gregory VII definitively confirmed the verdict of the Council and left him no hope of any future appeal.[12]

Instead of taking advantage of this generous offer of the Pope, Manassès continued his duplicity and tried to remain at the head of the Church of Rheims in spite of everything. On December 27, 1080, his patience and kindness exhausted, Gregory VII wrote four letters that brought this deplorable conflict to a conclusion.[13] He deposed Manassès once and for all, this time with no hope of reinstatement. He directed the clergy and the people of Rheims to resist the Archbishop, to expel him, and, with the legate's consent, to proceed with new elections. The Pope asked Count Ebal to stand by those who resisted Manassès and to support the new archbishop who would be elected. The Pope released the suffragan bishops of Rheims from all obedience to the excommunicated metropolitan and charged them with electing an archbishop worthy of the See of Rheims. Finally, he wrote a paternal and decisive letter to the King of France, Philip I:

> Saint Peter directs you and Gregory entreats you to give no further protection to Manassès, who has been definitively deposed for crimes that are not unknown to you, to withdraw your friendship from him, and no longer permit his presence in your court. By breaking with the enemies of the Church you will show that you love the Lord and, following these apostolic directives, that you sincerely desire to obtain the good graces of Saint Peter. By the apostolic authority with which We are invested, We forbid any obstacle to be placed in the way of the regular election of a new archbishop, which the clergy and people must hold. We request that you oppose anyone who would wish to place any obstacle and to

[12] *Epistolæ*, lib. VII, ep. XX, PL 148, 563.

[13] *Epistolæ*, lib. VIII, ep. XVII, XVIII, XIX, XX, PL 148, 590–94.

> give your protection to the one who will be chosen by the clergy and the people. . . . [The Pope dared to add:] This is an opportunity for you to show it was not in vain that We have been patient with the faults of your youth and hoped for your conversion.

More interested in his pleasures than in the religion of his kingdom, Philip I took no action against Manassès. The Archbishop remained a while longer in the See of Rheims. But his scandals and plunderings finally caused the people to rise up against him and drive him out of Rheims. According to Guibert of Nogent, Manassès found refuge with the excommunicated Emperor of Germany, Henry IV, attaching himself to one of the greatest enemies of the Church and the papacy. No more was heard of him.

With the departure of Manassès the exiles could return to Rheims. They were welcomed enthusiastically by the clergy and the people. Bruno especially received public honor: events had brought him to their attention. Although he did not take back his chair, or his title of director of studies, or the office of chancellor, the whole Church of Rheims favored him when the election of a new archbishop came up. One of the *Eulogies* describes the people's opinions of Bruno in this regard:

> Bruno had the approval of the city. He was the consolation and the pride of the people. Everything was in his favor, and we preferred him to anyone else. Our choice was right, because Brunc was a good man; but, although he was expert in every branch of learning, eloquent, and very wealthy, he disdained everything for the sake of Christ, undertook to follow Christ alone, and went to the wilderness with several followers.[14]

[14] *Titre* no. 52, Métropole de Rheims, PL 152, 570.

So, at the age of fifty, Bruno saw a wonderful future before him. The foremost episcopal See of France, the diocese that was called "the crown of the kingdom", was offered to him. Everything pointed to Bruno for this high office: his perfect integrity, his learning, his clarity of vision in delicate situations, his courage in trials, his faithfulness to the Holy See, his deep spirituality, his cultured sense of friendship, his detachment from riches, and his charity. Gregory VII and his legate, Hugh of Dié, had been able to appreciate his integrity during this period of simony, and they had publicly expressed the esteem in which they held him.

Who could oppose the election of this man whom everyone favored not only for the good of the Church of Rheims but for the good of the Church of France? Who? In reality, no one. Except God, who had already made his call to a more perfect life heard in Bruno's heart. It was not just in the Church of Rheims, nor even in the Church of France only, but it was at the very heart of the Church that Bruno would give his testimony of pure love for God.

IV

From the Garden of Adam's House to Sèche-Fontaine

Writing some twenty years later to his friend Raoul le Verd, who was provost of the Chapter at Rheims between 1096 and 1110, Bruno gives us a special insight into his vocation:

> You remember that day when we were together—you, Fulco le Borgne, and I—in the little garden beside Adam's house, where I was staying. We talked for some time, I think, about the false attractions and the perishable riches of this world and about the joys of eternal glory. With fervent love for God we then promised, we vowed, we decided soon to leave the fleeting shadows of the world to go in search of the good that is everlasting and receive the monastic habit. We would have carried out our plan promptly had Fulco not gone to Rome, but we put it off until he would return. He delayed, other reasons came up, his courage cooled, and his enthusiasm waned.

This account is the more wonderful because reliable documents about the life of Saint Bruno are rare. Here is an undeniable testimonial about one of the most important moments that determined the direction of Bruno's life. We shall often return to this disclosure for the purpose of appreciating what is in it, and, in a more general way, to the letter to Raoul le Verd as well. But what it does not say should also be noticed.

In the first place, Bruno says nothing to suggest when that conversation occurred. "The little garden beside Adam's house" surely refers to the area where the canons of Rheims had their houses. The conversation would then have taken place either before the canons went into exile at Count Ebal's or after their return. It is not likely that it was before, or what would have prevented Bruno from carrying out his plan then? Neither is there anything to confirm the hypothesis that it came after the exile. The text includes a little phrase that is both significant and mysterious. At the time of their meeting, Bruno was "a guest" at Adam's house (*ubi tunc hospitabar*). As a guest he was somewhat settled and not just paying a visit. Adam was not present at the meeting, and Bruno was free to receive his two friends, of whom one, Fulco, could be Adam's own brother.[1] All of this seems to indicate that the conversation did not occur at Rheims, but someplace where Bruno had been received as a guest for some reason we do not know—perhaps a rest, a trip, or exile.

It is therefore unwise to set a date too precisely for this important spiritual discussion between Bruno, Raoul le Verd, and Fulco le Borgne. The only thing to be said for certain is that the circumstances were such that, had it not been for Fulco's trip to Rome, the three friends would have forsaken the world soon after their meeting at Adam's house (*in vicino*).

This uncertainty about the date, though it does not weaken

[1] Concerning Fulco, cf. *Lettres des premiers Chartreux*. I. App. III, pp. 249–50.

the intrinsic value of the document in the least, nevertheless presents some difficulties for any biographer who would like to see in that decision an opportunity to understand the psychology of Bruno, perceive his motives, and record, so to speak, the effect of grace within him. The conversation of the three friends, and particularly of Bruno speaking about "the false attractions and the perishable riches of this world and the joys of eternal glory", about "the fleeting shadows of the world" and "the good that is everlasting", as well as their promise, their vow, and their decision—this is not all of equal importance for us. What he meant by those words depends upon when he spoke them: whether the three friends were still peacefully enjoying their wealth and their canonical livelihoods at Rheims or were in exile and deprived of their offices and their possessions or had at last regained all their honors and resources after the fall of Bishop Manassès. About Bruno himself the question will be even more specific: Was he then chancellor and director of studies for Rheims, or was he then—along with the Provost and some of the canons, or with Ponce only and not the Provost—still with the deceiving Archbishop; or was he at the point of being chosen archbishop of Rheims? The answer to these questions (if one can be given) will require an interpretation of the conversation in Adam's little garden, as well as the history of grace in Bruno's soul.

Unfortunately there is only the text of the letter, and to assign a date to the conversation is not possible.[2]

[2] Many biographies of Saint Bruno connect his vocation with an event that would have occurred in Paris and that Saint Bruno would have witnessed while he was a student. A doctor of the university, to whom some give the name Raymond Diocrès, sat up in his coffin three times during his own funeral saying he was damned. Though it has been accepted by some prominent people, among whom was Lesueur with his famous gallery of

"With fervent love for God we then promised, we vowed, we decided soon to leave": a threefold vocation so suddenly proposed that it seems to preclude—at least for Bruno, whose balance, wisdom, and gravity are so well known—his having made such an important decision, and confirming it with a vow, without first weighing it and allowing it to mature before God. Either that or he and his two friends must have experienced a truly extraordinary moment of grace—which, of course, is not impossible. But, had that happened, his narration would probably have given some hint of it.

The conversation that Bruno related is a climax in the story of his vocation, one of those important and significant moments, one of those powerful times that make it possible to study the interior landscape of a soul and follow its various pathways.

For Bruno and his two companions this was a moment of "fervent love for God" (*divino amore ferventes*) when they committed themselves to leave everything "to search for the good that is everlasting". But Bruno would not have responded to this fervor had not divine grace already prepared him for it. It would be surprising if the meeting in Adam's garden took place before the group of "resistance" canons went into exile at Count Ebal's; but even so, the date could not reasonably be placed after 1076. At this period everything in the life of Bruno indicated and confirmed his orientation toward *seeking God alone*. Faced several times with serious choices in his life, he had resolutely chosen God without compromise: he had dedicated his youthful and adult years to studying and then teaching the holy books, he

---

twenty-two paintings of the life of Saint Bruno, this anecdote has to be positively pronounced a legend totally unconnected with the life of Saint Bruno.

entered the clergy, and he became a canon of the cathedral of Rheims. While there he had demonstrated the virtues that are known through the *Eulogies*, because many of them were contributed by persons or groups who knew Bruno only before he left for Sèche-Fontaine, and from them it is possible to draw a sketch in which—allowing for hagiographic exaggeration—his face appears authentic and strong.

There is a contrast in his personality. Bruno was renowned as a "teacher", but he was also a very good man, prudent, simple, and honorable. The "master" has been described above. Nearly all of the *Eulogies* sing his praises. The phrase "teacher of teachers" appears several times. He is the glory of teachers (*decus magistrorum*). Sometimes the praise is very bold: "He is the wise Psalmist and the clearest of philosophers" (*doctus psalmista, clarissimus atque sophista*); if one speaks of Bruno, Plato's glory vanishes; "not only did he surpass all the doctors, but he produced excellent doctors, never lesser ones; he was the doctor among the doctors and not merely among the lesser clergy" (*faciebat summos doctores, non instituendo minores; doctor doctorum fuit, non clericulorum*). Some expressions are almost impossible to translate, like *Lumen et ordo viæ ducentis ad alta sophiæ*, and *exemplar quoque veri*. This notion of "verity" appears frequently: Bruno was the *norma veri dogmatis,* so that with him one felt doctrinally secure, in true dogma. His word touched hearts rather than spirits. He was the "splendor of discourse" (*splendor sermonis*) and therefore "the light of religion" (*lux religionis*). "Through him so many persons became wise", says one of the authors of the *Eulogies*, "that my spirit fails and my pen is silent." The character of Bruno is in contrast with so much knowledge, so much success, so much renown.

First of all, his extraordinary goodness. In the poems dedicated to his memory, the word is like a refrain. "Good" (*bonus*) is almost an epithet for him: "Bruno, called the good". Friendship is a joy for him: "He loves to be loved" (*se cupiebat amatum*). We have already referred to Maynard de Corméry's wonderful testimonial to his fidelity.

To goodness he joined prudence. *Prudens* and *prudentia* are words that give a true picture of Bruno: prudence in his speech, coming through his words as remarkable understanding (*floruit in mundo vir prudens ore profundo*); prudence in his counsels and in his conduct, which created a kind of elevated moral climate around him (*informatio morum, decus et prudentia mundi, integritas morum*). Prudence conferred upon him a place of honor in the city of Rheims (*major in urbe*).

All of this was combined with unusual simplicity (*vir simplex, simplex ut agnus*), as it appears many times in the *Eulogies*, a simplicity expressed by his manner of life, and particularly at the moment he was leaving Rheims when he showed his detachment (*calcator opum*), so that he was remembered by those who knew him as a man who disdained riches and honor. Here again admiration created untranslatable poetic expressions (*pauper Bruno factus iter, quorum fuit ante magister*).

Another characteristic that seems to have struck those who observed Bruno while he was living at Rheims and at Count Ebal's was his "probity", a word that in Latin has a broad, rich meaning. He is a man of remarkable principle (*vir egregiæ probitatis*). Never was Bruno found lacking in principle, and this confers upon him a reputation for integrity, uprightness, balance, fidelity, honesty, which no ordeal, not even the conflict with Manassès, could overwhelm: "No misfortune troubled the equanimity of his spirit, and he was never unhappy." Truly, he was "God's just man".

Nothing could upset this balance between his fame as teacher and his moral life. It must have had its source in his faith, a living faith that filled him with love for God (*puræ pietatis amator*), with piety in the original sense of the word (*Ipse pius, simplex, plenus Deitatis amore, impiger et mundus fuit, omni dignus amore*). He was a master in his time; he was the man of God, because he was attached not to the things of the world but to the One who made the world (*Exit ex mundo Vir, mundi spretor, ad illum qui mundum fecit*). All this admiration can be summed up in a word: he was the honor of the clergy (*Totius cleri decus*).

To repeat, in these *Eulogies* allowance must be made for the literary genre and for poetic exaggeration. But a rereading of the 178 *Eulogies* compels awareness of the tonality and especially dominant notes, particularly since among the *Eulogies* the most touching, the most moving are precisely those that express what they wish to say not in poetic form but in simple prose.

These *Eulogies* are evidence that Bruno was a spiritual light for his students. It was not just his learning or his profound thought that attracted the young people of the schools of Rheims to gather around his chair and bound him in friendship with so many of his contemporaries. It was his life, his person. From him they received "knowledge that turns into love".

In a phrase, very simple but rich and significant when one knows the bluntness of Hugh of Dié, the legate expresses what might be called Bruno's charism or particular grace: *Dominum Brunonem . . . in omni honestate magistrum*, which can be translated: "Master Bruno is master in all that gives honor" or "Master Bruno is master in everything that causes men to esteem a man."

These qualities of Bruno, which had been revealed earlier by his conduct while Gervais was bishop, evidently stood out in greater relief (by contrast, so to speak) after Manassès occupied the See of Rheims. Bruno *in omni honestate magis-*

trum stood in still greater contrast to that prelate, a simoniac and a deceiver, since the other Manassès, the provost of the canons, was not innocent of simony himself and had been publicly accused of it. Bruno could not be unaware of the situation in which he found himself, even—in spite of himself—mixed up in. He must have suffered profoundly not only because of his love of poverty, charity, justice, and integrity but also because of his love for the Church. To the moral poverty of Manassès I, the corruption of the gospel spirit in an archbishop who was responsible for one of the most important churches of France, the virtuous, incorruptible Bruno could react only by resisting or by withdrawing into a more virtuous life. First he chose to fight; but when everything was virtually the same after the fight, his experience of human mediocrity prompted him to try to find the purity of Christian life in solitude and with some chosen friends. In the Church of the eleventh century the most conscientious souls were attracted to some form of solitude.

The need to flee from Rheims to the lands of Count Ebal, the new boldness of Archbishop Manassès, the subterfuges by which Manassès succeeded in delaying the blow that threatened him, all the intrigues—these had to confirm Bruno in his plans. The more serious the situation became, the more he felt obliged to fight, while at the same time he was being drawn to solitude. This division within him reached a climax about the end of 1079, when the provost Manassès agreed to be reconciled with the Archbishop, taking with him all of the canons in exile except Bruno and Ponce, as the *Apologia* tells us. To stay with Ponce in exile, resisting the Archbishop, who was again giving the appearance of reconciliation with Rome and of victory over everyone who opposed him. What a case of conscience that was! But Bruno was too clearminded to fall into the Archbishop's trap, too honorable to accept anything that would make him seem to agree or even to compromise. He refused. At the risk of losing once and for all his property, his friends, his students, his church, and perhaps the esteem of the Pope, he refused. It was a radical choice, an absolute choice, one that had to weigh heavily upon Bruno's heart. To dare by himself to confront a prelate who had just vindicated himself in Rome before the Pope, a prelate who extended his offer of reconciliation with seeming sincerity—that was proof of an exceptional love of truth, justice, and honor. Here was a man who already knew how to be content possessing only God. For him solitude was not exile: solitude was living totally in faith and love. "Her deserts he shall make like Eden, her wasteland like the garden of the Lord; joy and gladness shall be found in her, thanksgiving and the sound of song."[3]

Given Bruno's attractive personality, refusing the See of Rheims may have been more difficult than breaking with the victorious Archbishop. But his conscience had to face the choice in a different form. He had struggled for justice and truth. Once Manassès was driven from Rheims, that struggle was over for him. Now that circumstances were favorable, he had to fulfill the vow he had made in Adam's little garden and go away into a new solitude, into monastic solitude, into the solitude of the wilderness.[4]

History has no record of how he left Rheims. Some biographers say that, because he escaped the episcopacy, he had

[3] Isaiah 51:3.

[4] Unfortunately, when Bruno refused it, the See of Rheims was again purchased, a sum of money being paid to the King of France by Hélinand, bishop of Laon. Hélinand was obliged to return to his former bishopric. Renaud du Bellay, treasurer of Saint Martin of Tours, succeeded him, and he would be followed in turn by the former provost Manassès.

to "flee" the city secretly.[5] Others, whose statement unfortunately seems to have no foundation, say he distributed all his property among the poor before he left and took his leave of the clergy and the people of Rheims in a magnificent sermon. "He commented upon the maxim he had adopted: 'In my spirit I have had eternal years, I have taken flight, and I have lived in the solitude.' He spoke with so much force, so much eloquence and so much authority, and the impression he made was so appealing and profound, that some of his hearers were ready to follow him. History mentions, among others, Peter of Béthune and Lambert of Bourgogne, who took the place of Fulco and Raoul le Verd."[6]

What is certain is that in refusing the archiepiscopal See of Rheims, which had been offered to him, and in choosing solitude and "the things of eternity" instead, Bruno was fully aware of his motive. He had experience of what he was leaving behind. What an experience! There is no doubt that the disturbing crisis in Rheims was the background for the seemingly severe words he addressed to Raoul le Verd: "Do not allow yourself to be delayed by deceitful riches—they cannot relieve our poverty; nor by the dignity of the provost's office—it cannot be exercised without great peril to the soul. Permit me to say that it would be repugnant and unjust to appropriate for your own use the possessions of which you are merely the administrator, not the owner. If the desire for honor and glory inclines you to live in style—

[5] Guibert of Nogent, *De vita sua*, bk. 1, chap. 10.

[6] Berseaux, *La Chartreuse de Bosserville*, p. 57. The text is taken from Psalm 55, "Appeals of one who is persecuted". If the anecdote is authentic, Bruno's choice of this text would be very significant, because several passages of the psalm can be applied to him: "And I say: Had I but wings like a dove, I would fly away and be at rest. Far away I would flee; I would lodge in the wilderness." But in fact the authenticity is doubtful.

and you cannot afford those expenses on what you possess —do you not in one way or another deprive some people of what you give to others?" The whole story of the episcopacy of Manassès can be heard in this advice. In a certain sense, in fact, it is the story of a great part of the Church during this period.

What were Bruno's intentions when he made the vow with his two companions in Adam's little garden, and later when he left Rheims? What kind of life had he decided to take up? Did he already have a clear plan? For an answer to this question there are only the words of the letter to Raoul le Verd, which he wrote more than ten years after he moved to the Chartreuse: *Disposuimus . . . fugitiva sæculi relinquere et æterna captare, necnon monachicum habitum recipere.* If we remember that this last phrase simply means "to embrace the monastic life" without specifying whether it would be the cenobitic or the eremitic form, the letter to Raoul le Verd provides only two points of the plan of Bruno and his companions: they intended to "flee the passing things of the world and to possess the eternal", that is, they intended to leave every secular occupation and relationship so they could dedicate themselves to God's life of grace.

Of course, it would be good to know whether, after leaving Rheims and especially after the conversation in Adam's garden, Bruno had specified which kind of life he would follow in the Chartreuse. That knowledge would shed light upon the "Sèche-Fontaine period" during his journey to the Chartreuse (more about that below), but just so much is known and no more. Documents from Sèche-Fontaine will clarify his plan. One thing is certain: Bruno would not choose a form of monastic life that would leave him in contact with the "passing things of the world" or one whose obligations would keep him from "possessing the eternal". The very simplicity of these two expressions reveals a determined desire for the absolute, which eliminates from his plan anything that would compromise the purity of the monastic life.

At a date that cannot be given precisely, but somewhere between 1081 and 1083, Bruno left Rheims with two companions, Peter and Lambert. They went straight south in the direction of Troyes. Some 150 kilometers [93 miles] from Rheims, 40 kilometers southeast of Troyes, was the abbey of Molesmes, which had existed since the end of 1075, and whose abbot, Robert, was renowned for his wisdom and holiness. Robert had gathered around him some hermits who were living in the forest of Collan, close to Tonnerre, and formed them in the Benedictine life. The abbey was poor. In 1083 the Lord-Bishop of Langres had to launch an appeal to his vassals to save Molesmes from poverty. That poverty fostered the fervor of the monks. When Bruno, Peter, and Lambert arrived there, a property called Sèche-Fontaine had recently been donated to the abbey of Molesmes but had not yet been used. It was located eight kilometers from Molesmes, far enough that its occupants could feel separate from the Benedictines of Molesmes, yet close enough that relations with the abbey and especially with its holy Abbot were easy. The forest of Fiel, which surrounded Sèche-Fontaine, was very suitable for the eremitical life. Individual hermits or groups of hermits had already found shelter in several places. By an agreement with Robert, Bruno and his companions settled at Sèche-Fontaine. There they followed the eremitical life (*heremitice vixerant*), says one of the two documents of Molesmes that relate the beginnings of Sèche-Fontaine.[7]

[7] There are two ancient documents concerning Bruno's stay at Sèche-

How long did this phase of Bruno's life last? Three years at the most, one year at least, depending upon the date of his departure from Rheims. In either case, it was long enough for other followers to join them, long enough also for their spiritual and temporal relationship with the abbey of Molesmes to influence their manner of life.

So wonderfully led by Robert, the abbey of Molesmes grew. It attracted the hermits who had settled nearby in the forests and influenced them to live together, and it established priories in the vicinity to provide a dwelling for its many candidates. It was inevitable that a day would come when, because of its growth, Molesmes would present the hermits of Sèche-Fontaine with the choice between a cenobitic life attached to the abbey and the eremitic life. The choice was not long in coming, and the hermits, together with the candidates who had joined them, were divided about the decision they should take. Peter and Lambert chose Molesmes. They stayed on the property at Sèche-Fontaine, where they built a church on the model of a Benedictine priory. The church was solemnly dedicated by the Bishop of Langres in 1086 along with other buildings of the community.[8] It was a free decision, wise, taken under the impulse

Fontaine. One was discovered by Mabillon; the other was uncovered in a search undertaken by P. de Tracy. They are still in the archives of the Côte d'Or in Dijon. The first dates from the first half of the twelfth century. The second, which is an original note rather than, strictly speaking, a document, dates from the end of the eleventh century. Our present understanding that Bruno stayed at Sèche-Fontaine as a hermit rather than as a Benedictine is based on a detailed examination of these two documents.

[8] What became of Peter and Lambert? There are two hypotheses. (1) They joined Bruno later, Peter being that Peter of Béthune who was the third prior of the Chartreuse (1100–1101), and Lambert becoming the third "Master of the Hermitage" at Calabria (+ 1124). (2) Peter became the abbot

of the Holy Spirit, like others of that time. Transferring from the life of a hermit to that of a cenobite, as well as going in the opposite direction, was not unusual.

But Bruno cherished a different ideal of religious life: the Spirit of God was sending him into solitude. He chose the way of the hermit, and so he, together with some companions, left Sèche-Fontaine and went in search of a place that would be suitable for his plan. The division took place with loyalty and charity. Robert and Bruno continued to have great esteem for each other.[9] When Bruno died in Calabria, the scroll went to Molesmes, and Molesmes wrote a warm tribute for the former hermit of Sèche-Fontaine. In the *Eulogy* that they dedicated to him (no. 40), the black monks called Bruno "our very good friend" (*familiarissimus noster*). Perhaps the hand of Robert himself can be detected in that superlative. Actually Robert, who had left Molesmes in 1098 and established Citeaux, returned to Molesmes[10] in 1099, where he must have remained until he died in 1110 or

---

of the Canons Regular of Saint-Jean-des-Vignes, near Soissons; Lambert, abbot of Pouthières in the diocese of Langres. In the present stage of research it is not possible to make any decision about these two hypotheses or, a fortiori, to choose between them.

[9] Some *Eulogies* declare that Bruno was first a monk and afterward a hermit. This leads to the conclusion that he was first a Benedictine of Molesmes and later a hermit in the Chartreuse and Calabria. That interpretation is incorrect. At that time the term *monk* included both "hermit" and "cenobite". The *Eulogies* indicate only that Bruno lived at Sèche-Fontaine for some time and later went to Chartreuse for the purpose of finding a stricter and deeper solitude there.

[10] The life of Saint Robert of Molesmes is a symbol of the fervor and the trials of eleventh-century monasticism. Born in 1028 or 1029, Robert entered the Benedictine abbey of Moutier-la-Celle near Troyes at the age of fifteen. After 1068 he was elected abbot of Saint-Michel-de-Tonnerre, in the diocese of Langres. In 1071, or later, he returned to Moutier-la-Celle. Then he was named prior of Saint-Ayoul-de-Provins. But the hermits in

1111. He was there when Bruno died in 1101 so he could add Molesmes' testimonial of great friendship to the funeral scroll.

By moving from Sèche-Fontaine, Bruno further clarified his vocation. As a monk he was not meant for the cenobitic life. He wanted solitude, to be "alone with the Alone" (*Mónos sun Mónô*), solitude with God. That is the call he had been hearing from the Holy Spirit.

He made his way south again and traveled more than 300 kilometers [186 miles] to Grenoble and the Alps. The reason for his choice is not known.[11] The only suggestion that might be likely is that Bishop Hugh of Grenoble and Bruno knew of each other and held each other in high regard, though they had never met. Hugh had been beside the Pope's legate Hugh of Dié at the Council of Lyons at the beginning of 1080 when Archbishop Manassès of Rheims was brought to trial and deposed, and Bruno's name must

---

the forest of Collan who wished to become cenobites chose him, with the approval of the Pope, to be their abbot. With them Robert founded Molesmes on December 20, 1075. After 1084, disturbed by the increasing riches of Molesmes, Robert and others withdrew to a nearby solitude. Later Molesmes called him back. Finally, in 1098, Robert and twenty-one monks who wanted to live the rule of Saint Benedict more strictly withdrew from Molesmes again and founded Citeaux. In 1099 Robert was again called back to Molesmes. There he died in 1111.

[11] Some authors attribute Bruno's decision to go to Grenoble to the influence of Seguin, the abbot of La Chaise-Dieu. This hypothesis has long been recognized to be erroneous. A still more persistent legend should also be rejected, the one that claims that Hugh was a disciple of Bruno at Rheims. When Bruno was studying at Rheims, Hugh was not yet born; when Bruno was named director of studies for Rheims, Hugh was only five years old (he was born in 1052). Hugh could have been Bruno's pupil toward the end of his professorship, but, if that were so, how is it that Guigo says nothing about it in his *Life of Saint Hugh*? Besides, the manner in which this hypothesis has been circulated makes it very doubtful.

have been spoken frequently in the presence of the young Bishop of Grenoble. Then, too, attentively following everything that the legate Hugh of Dié was doing, Bruno heard about Hugh of Grenoble and about the young bishop's courageous struggle to reform his diocese according to the views of Gregory VII and his legate. With his usual brevity, Guigo gives us the reason that induced Bruno to seek a hermitage in the forests of the Dauphiné: "Attracted by the gentle example of the saintly life of the holy Bishop Hugh of Grenoble, Bruno and his companions went to be near him" (*suavi sanctæ conversationis ejus odore trahente [ad virum sanctum Hugonem] venerunt [Bruno et socii ejus]*).

Toward the beginning of June 1084, Bruno and his six companions arrived at Grenoble. A wonderful and mysterious adventure was beginning for them.

V

The Solitude of Chartreuse

"In the year 1084 after the Birth of the Lord, the fourth year of the episcopate of Hugh, Bishop of Grenoble, Master Bruno and his brothers began to inhabit and to build the foundations of this hermitage, whose boundaries we have just specified."[1] A critical study of the documents indicates they took up residence there near the feast of Saint John the Baptist, which would be in the latter half of June. The climate, too, would prescribe that season of the year.

In his *Life of Saint Hugh* of Grenoble, Guigo recounted the arrival of Bruno and his companions. The narration is more concise than we might wish, but it is very exact.

> The leader was Master Bruno, renowned for his religious fervor and his learning, a model of virtue, dignity, and maturity. His companions were Master Landuino (who was prior of Chartreuse after Bruno); Stephen of Bourg and Stephen of Dié (formerly canons of Saint Ruf, who joined Bruno with the consent of their Abbot because of their desire for the solitary life); and then Hugh, whom they appointed their chap-

[1] The charter of the foundation of the Grande Chartreuse, officially promulgated by Bishop Hugh of Grenoble at the synod of December 9, 1086, at Grenoble. Cf. Bernard Bligny, *Recueil des plus anciens actes de la Grande Chartreuse (1086–1196)*, Grenoble, Allier, 1958.

lain, the only one who exercised the ministry of a priest;[2] and two laymen, Andrew and Guérin, whom we would now call brothers (*conversi*). They were looking for a place suitable for a hermitage and had not yet found one. Hoping to find it at last, they came to see Hugh, desiring to enjoy some spiritual conversation with him as well. He received them with joy and respect. He looked after them and helped them fulfill their vow. With his personal advice, assistance, and guidance they entered the solitude of the Chartreuse and settled there.

About this time Hugh had a dream. He saw God building a dwelling place for his glory in this solitude, and there were seven stars showing him the way. Seven! Bruno and his companions numbered exactly seven.[3] So he welcomed the plans of this first group as well as those who came later, and he gave the hermits the benefit of his counsel and generosity until he died.

This text is not entirely satisfying. It leaves uncertainty about several points of interest. It does not say, for example,

[2] Much has been written about these few words: *Eo quod solus ex eis sacerdotiis fungeretur officio*. Do they mean that Hugh was the only one of the group who was a priest or simply that he was appointed to exercise the priestly ministry for the community? No one should presume to make a final decision in this debate. As regards Bruno, it does not seem possible to claim that he was a priest: the testimony of the necrology of Chartreuse cannot be doubted. Chapter 15 of the customary, in regard to the election of a new prior, states this: "On the fourth day the monks assemble in Chapter, and, with the counsel of the oldest and the wisest, they choose from among them a priest or one who will be promoted to the priesthood."

[3] "At the beginning of the [Carthusian] Order the only symbol on the seal of the Grande Chartreuse was the Cross. The orb surmounted by the Cross appeared in the thirteenth century. . . . It was only during the seventeenth century that the stars over the orb and cross began to appear on seals and sculptures. They were still not in general or even very frequent use before the eighteenth century. . . . The inscription *Stat Crux dum volvitur orbis* appears for the first time about 1600 [and it] was little used before the nineteenth century." *La Grande Chartreuse par un Chartreux*, 12th edition, p. 36.

whether Bruno's companions came from Sèche-Fontaine with him. Most probably they did, because the idea of a totally solitary hermitage was not Bruno's ideal for religious life. Perhaps one or more joined the group on the way. It is possible, too, that the two canons from Saint Ruf did not meet Bruno until the day he stopped at the Saint Ruf priory near Saint-André on the way from Sèche-Fontaine to Grenoble. Regardless of what Guigo's text omits, however, it is still valuable.

Guigo confirmed that Bruno did not know where his hermitage would be until after he arrived at Grenoble. He was only "in search of a place suitable for the eremitic life". His concept of the eremitic life was clear, but he did not know where he would establish it. He "hoped" to find the place in Hugh's diocese, where there were many mountains and forests, but he was not certain that he would. On the other hand, he was sure that he would find Hugh to be a genuine man of God, one who would understand his plan, one whose support and conversation, like those of Robert of Molesmes, would encourage his enthusiasm.

Finally, if Bruno and his companions settled in the wilderness of the Chartreuse, it was not they who chose it. God himself, through Bishop Hugh, made that decision, though the Bishop's prophetic dream resists the most exacting critical analysis. Here Guigo is a firsthand witness, because he was a friend and confidant of Hugh of Grenoble for twenty-six years. His information came directly from the Bishop. To the historian, too, Guigo appears to be a perfect witness, critical and trustworthy. His sincerity is beyond question. He is always careful and prudent. He had serious reservations about miracles. In his *Life of Saint Hugh*, which he undertook at the request of Pope Innocent II, he described a holy life without mentioning a miracle. If he related the dream about the seven stars, it was because he could not disbelieve it. No one could reject it without declaring a priori that any kind of unusual mystical phenomenon was impossible. The events that followed, the entire spiritual history of the Carthusian Order, show how the landscape influenced the shape of Carthusian life. Between the landscape and the life there was a profound and determining relationship.

The little band left the house of the Bishop of Grenoble one June morning in 1084 and started on the way through Sappey and the Porte Pass toward Saint-Pierre de Chartreuse. They went beyond the pass at the entrance to the wilderness and continued all the way to the extreme end of the narrow valley of the Chartreuse.[4] Did Bruno and his companions go to the far end of the gorge because of the dozen springs that were there? But there were still more productive springs in the valley, like the beautiful and abundant spring of Mauvernay, the one that made Guigo choose the location of present-day Chartreuse.

There is no proof the spring was miraculous. Miraculous springs belong to the folklore of sanctity. But this area, this climate, this atmosphere, this rhythm of seasons and temperatures that Bruno appreciated and desired—these were very important: in a way that nothing else does, they reveal his plan.

Standing out in bold relief, just like the sun, his plan can be seen in the whole landscape, in the forest and the snows. The end of the gorge in the heart of the mountains of Chartreuse, with access difficult even from the nearest villages, with long winters, deep snow, and poor soil—that was an

[4] Chartreuse was the proper name of the wilderness before Bruno and his six companions came and settled there. The reputation of the hermitage enlarged the original sense of the word until it came to designate the mountains all around it. Then people spoke about "the mountains of Chartreuse".

advantage for him, creating an almost complete separation from the world, the utmost solitude. Here was the austere hermitage for which Bruno was looking. But it was a hermitage for several hermits: one man completely alone could not survive in conditions like those. Since Bruno agreed to make his "earthly dwelling" there, he had to have a plan in which the spiritual and human ties of the group would balance the considerable risks that solitude entails.

Bruno did not arrive at Chartreuse all alone. He was leading six companions, whom he had already formed into a remarkably united and harmonious group of like-minded men. The two "masters", Bruno and Landuino, guaranteed doctrinal nourishment—solid, substantial food drawn from the Holy Scriptures—for these men who had vowed themselves to the contemplative life: two laymen, Andrew and Guérin, who, leading a solitary life as much as possible like that of the hermits, relieved their thousand material and physical needs and so freed them for pure prayer, which they shared as much as they could; and finally, at least one who was a priest, who exercised the priestly ministry for the group and was called "the chaplain", a word that implies a community. The contrast between the austerity of the hermitage and the close harmony of the little group of hermits provides an insight into Bruno's plan. If he had not seen that he could achieve this kind of hermitage in the wilderness of Chartreuse, he surely would not have settled there. But this place fitted his plan too well for him to hesitate: there he and his six companions could hope to live the eremitic life with all its demands and all its richness, insofar as human powers were capable.

However, the wilderness of Chartreuse was going to have a strong and lasting influence upon the accomplishment of that plan.

The 1086 document of donation indicates the boundaries of the area that was granted to the hermits:

> The boundaries of the solitude that we have been given pass below the area called the Cluse and follow the boulder that closes that valley to the east, following the ridge that closes and divides Combe-Chaude, and extends to the middle of the monolith above Bachais;[5] then another dry ridge that goes down to the mountain of Bovinant; from there another ridge that goes down from Bovinant at the edge of the forest to the boulder below la Follie; then the monolith that goes from la Follie to Mount Alliénard and that goes down from Alliénard toward the Morte on the west side to the monolith of Cordes, which extends toward Perthuis. The boundaries then follow the ridge of the monoliths to the river called Guiers-Mort, which serves as the boundary as far as the Cluse.

This description gives an impression of the Chartreuse area: a place surrounded by mountains with a single pass called the Cluse. Here and there, especially at the lowest part of the valley, limestone soil covered a narrow stratum of humus, where trees forming a wooded area clung to the soil that lacked depth. In this rocky place there was an occasional meadow to feed some cattle. It was useless to dream about planting vines or grain or fruit trees in this soil. The altitude and the climate precluded that. By working the soil diligently it was possible to grow a few vegetables. For contemplatives to settle in this wilderness was to dedicate themselves to austerity. They were compelled to live frugally. It was not possible to make use of the trees because there were no roads for removing them. The Carthusians were not able to profit from the forest until the seventeenth century. For

[5] Bachais, which means a "boat", is derived from the word for ferry and, in the old dialect, signified a drinking trough.

their livelihood they depended on a little agriculture and some flocks. Iron was discovered in the mountains later.

For many years it seemed unrealistic to think this wilderness could sustain more than thirty people, and it was better to have more "brothers" than "fathers", more laborers than contemplatives. When he edited the *Customs*, Guigo set the size of the community at thirteen fathers and sixteen brothers. When the Carthusians of Chartreuse wanted to increase their number, they had to acquire land farther down the mountain, toward the plain. Here is one of the original characteristics of the Chartreuse. It was not the sort of hermitage, flourishing at that time, that the Camaldolese were building around a monastery of cenobites. Bruno wanted a hermitage strictly speaking: that is, total solitude, mitigated only by a little bit of communal living. They would be few, and even in their common life the hermits would preserve the feeling of being a "small number".

The climate, especially the heavy snowfall in Chartreuse and the severe cold, imposed on Bruno a decision about the environment. There were two ways to combine the requirements of solitude and those of the regular life: one was to ensure solitude by placing the cells as far from each other as possible; the other was to promote their common life by placing them in groups. The climate persuaded Bruno to compromise: the cells would be completely separated but near each other and connected to each other and the areas for common life by a covered cloister, so that they would have a sheltered walk from one place to another during rain and snow. He intended for them to be called together frequently, several times a day, whether for one of the Hours, or for a Chapter meeting, or for meals together. If the environment had not suited his plan for contemplative life, Bruno could have changed the arrangement of the huts without leaving the wilderness of Chartreuse. For example, he put the brothers a mile and a half from the cells of the hermits, 1,000 feet down the mountain, where the sun shines more often and the snow melts more quickly.

What Bruno had planned was very close to what he established at the Chartreuse, even if it was not exactly the same.

In at least two passages of his *Customs*, Guigo mentioned the bold establishment of the first hermitage. He asked that "no one criticize [the physical arrangements of the Carthusians] before living a sufficient time in a cell, among the heavy snows and the severe cold". In his view, nothing except experience of the contemplative life could explain and justify the bold foundation of Bruno and the first Carthusians. To understand and appreciate a hermitage like the one Bruno envisioned and established requires the grace of a vocation. The letter to Raoul le Verd explains something of the motives that induced Bruno to live in Chartreuse. More about that later.

Bruno and his companions built and organized their first dwelling. According to one tradition, the hermits received hospitality among the inhabitants of Saint Peter of Chartreuse the first few days after they arrived there. Bruno himself lived with the Brun family,[6] who provided the wood he needed to build his cell. They received other acts of generosity as well. Even today, after 900 years, the names of two of the inhabitants of Ruchère are mentioned: Molard and Savignon took the responsibility of baking bread for the first Carthusians and bringing it to them, which was no small service. They began to work as soon as they arrived

[6] F. de saint-Andéol, *L'archéologie au monastère de la Grande Chartreuse*, Grenoble, Allier, 1869, p. 6.

and continued diligently, because they had to arrange the essentials before the first snowfalls and before the cold came, so they had only about three months. While some of the land was being prepared for planting, hermitages were being built around the spring. They must have resembled little chalets, like the cabins of woodcutters or shepherds that are still seen in the mountain pastures, rustic but durable, made of logs and covered with sturdy boards, built to resist the weight of the yearly snows. Because of the lack of time and also, perhaps, of money, each of these dwellings sheltered two monks at first:[7] later everyone had a cell to himself. Water from the spring came to each of the cells by means of conduits, which at first were just hollowed-out trunks or branches of trees.

Only the church was built of stone. Bishop Hugh of Grenoble consecrated it on September 2, 1085, under the title of the Holy Virgin and Saint John the Baptist.[8]

This group of buildings may have been located near the present-day Saint Bruno chapel.

The cells opened onto a covered walk about thirty-five yards long, which went "almost to the foot of the mono-

[7] It was in *The Life of Saint Hugh* that Guigo mentions this practice of the first Carthusians. Some have wanted to see a trace of the influence of Saint Peter Damian and Saint Romuald and to attribute to Guigo the responsibility for changing from a cell for two monks to solitary ones. But an attentive study of the documents indicates rather that the reason for the cell for two was lack of space, and the practice lasted only a short time, not for twenty-five years.

[8] One tradition says that Bruno had a small oratory constructed apart from the new monastery, not far from the spring, where he used to go to pray. This would be the origin of the chapel that today is called the Saint Bruno chapel. Perched at the edge of a steep cliff, this oratory was spared from the avalanche of 1132. It was restored during the fifteenth century and rebuilt almost completely in 1610 by Jacques Danès de Marly, bishop of Toulon. It was again restored in 1816.

lith", permitting sheltered access to the chapter room, the refectory, and the church. In the church the hermits celebrated the conventual Mass and together recited Matins and Vespers on ordinary days and, on Sundays and feast days, the entire Office. They recited the rest of the Office in their cells on ordinary days. They occupied themselves with prayer, reading, and manual labor, the labor consisting mostly of classifying or transcribing manuscripts, especially the Bible and the Fathers of the Church. Each one took his meals alone. Only on Sundays and the great feast days did they go to the refectory, when one of the hermits would read some passage from the Bible or the Fathers while the community was eating.

The brothers lived within the boundaries of the wilderness, too, but their dwellings were located below the hermitages. They took care of the exterior works, especially the farm labors that were necessary for the community's subsistence. They cultivated the land, cared for the livestock, cut wood, and performed the thousand crafts that were required for the upkeep of the buildings. In short, they protected the prayer life and the solitude of the hermits while living, as much as possible, a contemplative life themselves.

The spiritual harmony of this group of men was remarkable. Each one in love with God, they merged their lives in a way that would free them for pure contemplation.

There are two valuable accounts that describe the life of the first Carthusians. One is by Guibert of Nogent; the other by Peter the Venerable, abbot of Cluny. Guibert of Nogent never visited the Grande Chartreuse, but he has information from eyewitnesses whose account is true. He describes the Chartreuse of 1114, when it was thirty-eight years old. Peter the Venerable wrote about 1150, but he was acquainted with the Chartreuse since 1120, when he was prior of the Benedictine priory of Domène, not far from Grenoble. Thereupon he began a friendly correspondence with the priors of the Chartreuse. Even after he left Domène he visited his friends of the wilderness several times, admiring their life. His account was a little later than Guibert of Nogent's, but it came from his personal experience. Here is what they wrote.

First, Guibert of Nogent described the place Bruno chose for his hermitage as "a high and formidable promontory (*promontorium*), reached by an extremely dangerous—one might say nonexistent—route". Then he continued:

> The hermits' church is built almost at the edge of the monolith. Beyond it arranged in a curve is a group of dwellings where thirteen monks are living. Their cloister is convenient enough for the practices of the cenobitic life, but they do not live in a cloistered community like other monks. . . . Within the precincts of the cloister each one has his own cell, where he works, sleeps, and eats. On Sunday he receives from the bursar his bread and vegetable for the week. Water for drinking and other purposes comes from the spring through a conduit that makes its round of the cells and supplies each one through an opening in it. On Sundays and solemn feast days they eat cheese and fish, when some good people bring it to them: they do not buy them. . . . When they drink wine, it is so diluted with water that it has lost its strength, being scarcely better than water. Their cloth of their monastic habits is of poor quality. They gather in the church at set times, which are not the same as ours. . . .
>
> They are ruled by a prior, with the Bishop of Grenoble, a very religious man, serving as their abbot. . . . They cultivate a little land for wheat, but the sale of the flocks they have assures their subsistence. . . . The place is called Chartreuse. . . . Below this mountain there is a group of dwellings where some twenty devout laymen live and work on their

own. These hermits, too, dedicate themselves to contemplation with so much fervor that they never deviate from their reason for being there, and, despite the austerity of their manner of life, the passing of time has not diminished their zeal. . . . Though they are poor, they have a fine library: one would say they work with so much zeal to acquire eternal nourishment that they need less by way of earthly nourishment.[9]

The account of Peter the Venerable essentially confirms the one of Guibert of Nogent:

Among all the European forms of our monastic foundations in the region of Burgundy, there is one that surpasses many of the others in holiness and spiritual valor. It was founded in our own time by some Fathers, wise and holy men of great courage: namely, master Bruno of Cologne, master Landuino of Italy, and some others, fine men, as I said, and God-fearing. . . . They fast almost continuously. . . . Like the Egyptian monks of old, they dedicate themselves constantly to silence, reading, prayer, and manual labor, especially copying books. In their cells, at the sound of the church bell, they pray part of the canonical Hours: namely, Prime, Terce, Sext, None, and Compline. For Vespers and Matins they all assemble in the church. . . . They change the daily routine on certain feast days . . . when they take two meals and, like the monks who are cenobites rather than hermits, they sing all of the Hours in the church,[10] and all without exception

[9] Guibert of Nogent tells a story that, if it is accurate, reveals the spirit of poverty that the first Carthusians possessed. Visiting the hermits of Chartreuse, the Count of Nevers marveled at the poverty of their life. He would have sent them some valuable silver pieces. The hermits thanked him, but they would not take his gift. They would accept only some leaves of parchment to use in their work of transcribing books.

[10] The author is mistaken here. Guigo declares in the *Customs* that "we always say Compline in our cell". That is still the practice of the Carthusians.

> go to the refectory for their meals, one after Sext, then again after Vespers. . . . They remain very recollected. They recite the Office with their eyes cast down toward the ground and their heart fixed upon heaven. By the gravity of their demeanor, the sound of their voice, and the expression on their faces they show they are totally—interiorly as well as exteriorly—absorbed in God. . . . The Carthusians practice great detachment, wishing to have nothing except what is prescribed.[11]

Mabillon recalled a tradition that Bruno used to like to withdraw to a solitary corner of the nearby forest and meditate before a monolith where a cross engraved in the rock can still be made out.

All these details give the vivid impression that there was a wonderful harmony between the kind of life that God had inspired in Bruno and the Chartreuse that he chose as the place to accomplish his plan. Anyone who believes in inspiration will see the hand of providence in this harmony. If Bruno's experience as a canon at Rheims is detected in certain practices, if his stay at Sèche-Fontaine and the influence of Bishop Hugh of Grenoble inclined him to adopt some Benedictine practices, if some details of observance or liturgy came from the Order of Saint Ruf or other Rules,[12]

[11] Peter the Venerable, *De miraculis*, bk. II, chap. 28, PL 189, 943 and 945.

[12] The study of the origins of the Carthusian liturgy is a source of admiration for the spirit and profound joy for the soul. This is not the place to describe it, though it would be interesting to know what the Mass and the Office were like for the first Carthusians. The authors of *Aux sources* write, "Our first Fathers made no changes. From the beginning they had to have an Office, and there were no Carthusian books, so they had to borrow books, though they surely did not use everything in them. That would have been too much for this small group of hermits." This period was followed by one of "more systematic elaboration" and then, with Guigo, a period of skillful, wise synthesis. "This liturgy, sober, bare, and simple, suitable

his plan, from the beginning of the Chartreuse, was nonetheless original, new, unique. In the *Mystica theologia*, edited by Hugh the Carthusian at the beginning of the thirteenth century, this plan was clearly drawn up. There were two main premises: Bruno and his companions wanted a hermitage whose dangers and inconveniences would be reduced by elements taken from cenobitic life. Those elements of community life were not a concession to human weakness but rather a way of combining the spiritual and the human. A holy friendship bound the members together, a friendship of strong personalities who were great, learned, and holy (*magnis, doctis, sanctis*), with Bruno the outstanding example.[13]

Three traits seem to characterize the Carthusian that Bruno envisioned: contemplation nourished by Holy Scripture and the Fathers; knowledge of Scripture and the Fathers stimulated by contemplation; and knowledge full of love, love that desires knowledge. The Carthusian lives the mystery of God in his spirit and his heart. And that "grandly": there was nothing stingy in this vocation—everything was arranged to convey their awareness of the absolute, of need, of totality, of completeness, which gives the man of God (*homo Dei*) his true stature.

The place, therefore, is important. Such an existence cannot be achieved just anywhere. The very setting has to be favorable. Wilderness is a requirement, as well as separation from the world, a limited number of hermits, and a proper

---

for the contemplative vocation of small communities of hermits, and still so pure, remains a precious jewel among the rites of the Church."

[13] In his discourse on *l'État des Lettres en France au XIIe siècle*, Dom Rivet says that Saint Bruno's first companions "were the wisest men of their time". *Hist. Litt.*, vol. IX, p. 119.

balance of "fathers" and "brothers". The Chartreuse offered a rare, perhaps unique, opportunity to reach that ideal without any compromise.

It cannot be known whether or in what degree, in their pursuit of that goal, Bruno and his companions had the idea of starting an Order. What they established was a hermitage, a limited hermitage, with specific requirements, in unique circumstances, a hermitage that they could hope would continue long after them. Their awareness of the originality of the foundation was too vivid (and especially their desire to be silent, to be humble, to be forgotten, and to deny themselves was too definite) for them to dream of expanding into other places and among other men. They had no thought of repeating their experience in another place or at another time. The first generation of Carthusians, and Bruno himself, lived and died with no intention except to live like perfect contemplative hermits, their ideal marked by its absolute purity. Afterward, God would make changes in ways they had not foreseen, but that would be God's affair. "They had come to seek God alone in the wilderness of Chartreuse", say recent historians concerning the beginning of the Carthusian Order. "They did not know what God was preparing through them and by them. Without their knowledge people, events, and things would modify the organization of their life in such a way that the Order of Carthusians would be born from the original seed with its own special character." Dom Le Masson would write one day: "They did not think that their humble sort of life (*vile suum propositum*, in Guigo's phrase) was a little trickle of water that was destined to become a great river. The question did not even occur to them (*imo nec de hac re cogitabant*)."

Did they bind themselves by a formal "profession" of vows? It is not clear that they did at first. In chapter 23 of his *Customs*, Guigo I describes the profession of a novice. The formula of vows, like the ceremony itself, was surprisingly sober and simple. Here is the original formula of vows: "I, brother ———, promise stability, obedience, and conversion of my life, before God and his saints and the relics in this hermitage, which has been erected in honor of God and of ever Virgin Blessed Mary and of Saint John the Baptist: in the presence of Dom ———, the prior." The formula of monastic profession, as it was used everywhere at the time, can be recognized in it, though without mentioning the Rule of Saint Benedict, and replacing the word *monastery* with *hermitage*. Earlier in the ceremony the prior blessed the professiant, who was bowing before him. The formula of blessing, several centuries older than the first Carthusians, was used among all monks. The choice of this one, though, is very interesting. There were four or five formulas for blessing the new professiant, and from those the first Carthusians kept the one that was the most scriptural, the most spiritual, showing again their special attachment to the Bible. Here is that formula with its beautiful overtones from the Gospel:

> Lord Jesus Christ, the only Way for anyone to come to the Father, we ask you in your unfailing love to lead this servant of yours, detached from desires of the flesh, by the way of regular discipline; and, since you were willing to call sinners, saying, "Come to me, all you who are burdened, and I will give you rest", grant that your invitation will become so strong that he will put down the burden of his sins, taste how good you are, and deserve to receive you as his nourishment. Number him among your sheep so that he will know you and follow no stranger, that he will not even hear the voice of other shepherds but only yours, saying, "If anyone would serve me, let him follow me." You who live and reign. . . .

If this liturgy did not yet exist at the time of Bruno, we may be sure at least, from all that we know of Guigo and his *Customs*,[14] that it faithfully reflects his spirit and the spirit of the first Carthusians.

The title of the hermitage of Chartreuse was mentioned in the profession of vows. It was "erected in honor of God and of the ever Virgin Blessed Mary and of Saint John the Baptist". These simple words indicate the special focus of Carthusian spirituality: God and the ever-virgin Mary who was the perfect example of a soul united to God, and John the Baptist, who was the precursor and man of the desert par excellence[15]—this focus came directly from the soul of Bruno.

In *Customs* there are additional texts taken from the Bible, and especially from the Gospel of our Lord. If they are not always quoted word for word, their spirit is everywhere. And since Guigo does not intend to hand on anything except "what we are accustomed to do at Chartreuse", they seem to be a conspicuous sign of the attraction that Holy Scripture had for Bruno and the first Carthusians right from the beginning.[16] The *Commentary on the Psalms* contains frequent references to the contemplative life. Here is the reverse: the contemplative life refers constantly to the sacred

[14] Guigo I drew up the *Customs* between 1121 and 1127. He undertook this task to satisfy the requests of some of the priors and in obedience to Hugh of Grenoble. In humility he took great care not to present himself as a legislator but to be content with the role of one recording the customs observed at the Grande Chartreuse, saying, "This is what we are accustomed to do."

[15] Saint John the Baptist is the secondary patron of the Carthusian Order.

[16] This attraction for the Bible is common to several monastic founders of the eleventh and twelfth centuries. Here it is sufficient to recall Saint Bernard. For Bruno and the first Carthusians the note sounds a little louder because of the sobriety and the brevity of the *Customs*.

texts. The movement is basically the same, however: the life, the breath, the work, the existence of the first Carthusians were in the context of the Bible. It was the dwelling place of his soul.

The most likely theory about the *Commentary on the Psalms* was presented earlier: if it was not written at Chartreuse, it was surely taken up, amended, and completed by Bruno there. Observing Bruno and his first companions settle and live in the Chartreuse recalls some passages of the *Commentary*, like that lengthy and solemn paraphrase on Psalm 118. This description of the "faithful and perfect ones", "those who search for God with all their heart", "who purify their path by observing his words", those anxious appeals to the One "who alone gives life", that intense feeling of being "only a guest on the earth", that joy of "having chosen the way of truth", that desire "to run the way of the Commandments", "of keeping them until the end", those earnest prayers to "obtain the grace of God", to "examine the words of God", that complete belonging to God alone, and so many other sentiments, like this: "How I love your law! I ponder on it all the day long"—what is that except the very breath of the first Carthusian?

Great satisfaction came to Bruno and his companions on December 9, 1086.[17] That day, in the synod that was being held at Grenoble, Bishop Hugh officially ratified the grant that the landowners of Chartreuse had made two years earlier. Not only did the Carthusians become lawful masters of the land, but the document solemnly reaffirmed the purpose of the hermitage:

[17] The charter of donation does not bear a date. It was the Bollandists who provided it, noting that the fifth of the Ides of December fell that year on the fourth feria of the second week of Advent, as indicated in the last clause of the charter.

> The grace and mercy of the holy and undivided Trinity has made us aware of the conditions of our salvation. Recalling our human condition and how inevitable sin is in this fragile life, we have judged it good to redeem ourselves from the hands of death, to exchange the goods of this world for those of heaven, to acquire an eternal heritage instead of possessions that will not last. We do not wish to incur the double sorrow of undergoing the miseries and labor of this life and then the eternal pains of the next.
>
> For that reason we make over an area of wilderness into the possession of Master Bruno and the brothers who have come with him in search of a solitude where they can live for God alone: I, Humbert of Mirabel, with my brother Odo and the others who have rights over this place; namely, Hugh of Tolvon, Anselm Garcin; Lucy and her sons Rostaing, Guigues, Anselm, Ponce and Boson, who are representing their mother; and likewise Bernard Lombard and his sons; as well as Seguin, the lord abbot of Chaise-Dieu, and his community, give all their rights over these lands to the above-mentioned hermits.

After giving a precise, legal description of the boundaries of the area, the document continues:

> If any powerful person tries to annul this grant in whole or in part, let him be considered guilty of sacrilege, separated from the communion of the faithful and burned in everlasting fire unless he repents and repairs the damage he has caused.
>
> Master Bruno and the brothers who were with him began to occupy the above-mentioned land in the year of our Lord 1084, the fourth of the episcopate of Bishop Hugh of Grenoble, who, with all his clergy, approves and confirms the grant made by the above-mentioned persons, and, insofar as he is concerned, surrenders all of his rights over that territory.

After listing the witnesses, the document concludes with the date: "The present charter has been read at Grenoble, in the Church of the Blessed and Glorious ever Virgin Mary, on the fourth feria of the second week of Advent, in the presence of the aforesaid Hugh, bishop of Grenoble, his canons, and many other persons, both priests and clerics, assembled in holy synod, the fifth of the Ides of December."[18]

This 1086 document of donation shows Bishop Hugh's favor and generosity toward the first Carthusians. His friendship never waned, and his influence was considerable, not only during the settlement of the hermits in the Chartreuse but during the first forty-eight years of the Order. His influence was also kind, based on admiration and affection more than on his canonical authority. Hugh was thirty-two years old and four years a bishop when Bruno and his companions arrived at Grenoble. He had tried everything to avoid becoming a bishop, but, because the legate Hugh of Dié had honored him and designated him, he finally had to submit. Hugh of Dié himself conferred upon him all of the orders except the episcopate. It was at Rome, in April or May of 1080, that the young man was consecrated Bishop of Grenoble by Pope Gregory VII.

Following the directives of the legate Hugh of Dié, he immediately undertook the struggle against the abuses that were afflicting the diocese and clergy of Grenoble. It was a relentless, tiring struggle for Hugh, and it revived his long desire to enter a monastery. One day he fled to Chaise-Dieu,

[18] Bernard Bligny, op. cit. Acte I, p. 3. Bishop Hugh asked only a little annual rent as a remembrance of the favors from the Church of Grenoble to the Carthusian Order. This rent consisted of fifteen small portions of butter and a fifth (100 kg. [220 lbs.]) of white cheese. The portions of butter were for the bishop, the senior, and the oldest of the canons; the cheese was distributed among the rest of the cathedral clergy. The Carthusians discharged this obligation until 1792. Cf. Barthelemy, *History of Grenoble*, ms. cited by M. A. du Boys, *Life of Saint Hugh*, p. 75 (*La Grande Chartreuse par un Chartreux*, p. 18).

and it took a formal order from Gregory VII to remove him from there. Nevertheless, after his return to Grenoble, his enthusiasm for monastic life remained; and, although he had no experience of it except for the Benedictine cenobitic life at Chaise-Dieu, Hugh immediately recognized Bruno's zeal, his ideals, his love for God, and his special gifts, which attracted Hugh and caused him to associate himself with the venture. There was a difference of twenty years in the ages of Hugh and Bruno, but the two men developed the deep friendship that is known by true men of God. In his *Life of Saint Hugh*, Guigo wrote: "With Hugh counseling, helping, accompanying, [Bruno and his companions] entered the solitude of Chartreuse and constructed" (*Ipso [Hugone] consulante, juvante, comitante, Cartusiæ solitudinem [Bruno et socii ejus] intraverunt et exstruxerunt*). Each one of these words should be considered. For the first Carthusians Hugh had the role of counselor, helper (one who assists and tries to encourage), and companion (one who makes his own the lot of those he accompanies). He had this role not only when they arrived at Chartreuse, but during the whole period of their settlement, organization, and construction of the buildings (*exstruxerunt*). Hugh liked to meet Bruno at Chartreuse, to converse with him, to be formed by him, to live near him.[19] Guigo reported that it was not unusual for Bruno himself to have to—in some way—"chase" (*compellerent exire*) Hugh from the wilderness, saying: "Go, go to your flock and discharge the obligations that you have toward them." During his more than fifty years as bishop, Hugh remained faithful

[19] Along with Bishop Hugh, William, the prior of Saint Laurence of Grenoble, sometimes came to the Chartreuse to make a retreat. In 1086 William was named abbot of Saint Chaffre in the diocese of Puy, and although he then had to give up his visits to Bruno, he always maintained a very strong friendship with him.

to the Carthusians. It was at his insistence that Guigo, the fifth prior of Chartreuse, wrote the *Customs* between 1121 and 1128; and, while he did that, Hugh, who had known Bruno, Landuino, Peter of Béthune, and John of Tuscany,[20] was present as an important link that guaranteed, in a way, that the Order would be faithful to the original thought of Bruno.

Guigo wrote: "Until his death Hugh never ceased to favor the men of Chartreuse with his counsels and charity." An anonymous manuscript from Mont Dieu, reflecting the tradition of the century following Hugh's death (+1132), characterized him in these words: "One may say that he was the patron and founder of the House of Chartreuse and the Carthusian Order and, although it was not at first his undertaking, in some way their creator" (*Vere dici potest et domus et Ordinis Cartusiensis patronus atque fundator, et quamvis non primus, tamen quodammodo institutor*). Guibert of Nogent (+1124) had used a more ambiguous phrase: "The Bishop of Grenoble filled the role of abbot and guardian" (*Vicus autem abbatis ac provisoris Gratianopolitanus episcopus . . . exsequitur*).[21] The "role of abbot" must not be taken in a juridical or canonical sense, because the Carthusians had no abbot but only priors. It was Hugh's complete dedication to the Carthusians that suggested that image to Guibert. His thought might be better expressed: "For them he was like an abbot and guardian." These phrases seem excessive only because they attempted to express a situation for which ordinary language has no exact words. Hugh's relationship with the Carthusians was like that of a patron, founder, creator, abbot, and guardian.

[20] These were the first priors of Chartreuse, preceding Guigo I.

[21] *De vita sua*, PL 156, 854.

That describes the spiritual and human environment in which Bruno and his companions lived during their first years at Chartreuse. All was providentially successful: Bruno's plan, the coming vocations, and even the personal desire of Hugh of Grenoble, all seemed to coincide perfectly. Bruno could believe that he had finally reached the harbor he had been seeking. For six years he led a life that appeared to him to be the purest, the holiest, the most dedicated, the most useful for a world in which even churchmen were corrupted by too much involvement in political and temporal affairs. He thought he had at last found in Chartreuse the solitude with God that was the prelude to seeing him face to face in eternity.

The people of the Dauphiné were not mistaken about the spiritual importance of what was happening in the Chartreuse. "In the beginning," wrote a seventeenth-century historian, "those saintly strangers were called hermits, and their leader, hermit par excellence. Their arrival opened a new era there. The history of that year can only be dated 'the year the hermit came'."[22] God was going to reveal to him and to all who know his life that there is a solitude still more profound than that of the wilderness: namely, the solitude of obedience and self-giving of those for whom it is chosen not by themselves but by God: "Another will bind you and lead you where you did not wish to go." Jesus' words to Peter were true for Bruno.

[22] Chorier, *General History of the Dauphiné*, Lyons, 1672, vol. II, p. 16. Quoted in *La Grande Chartreuse par un Chartreux*, 1976, p. 24, n. 26.

VI

Solitude in the Court of Pope Urban II

Pope Gregory VII died on May 25, 1085. After all his work and struggles, the Church he left was in a sorrowful, distressing state. Henry IV, Emperor of Germany, had unlawfully installed Guibert, the deposed archbishop of Ravenna, upon the throne of Saint Peter as Clement III. Guibert employed the military power of the empire against the lawful Pope. Before he died, Gregory VII had assembled the cardinals and some bishops who remained faithful to him, and he entreated them to choose as his successor a man with the character and virtue to continue the necessary internal reform of the Church and to resist the pressures of the antipope. He even suggested three names to them: Didier, abbot of Monte Cassino; Odo, bishop of Ostia; and Hugh, archbishop of Lyons.

Didier, abbot of Monte Cassino, was elected on May 24, 1086. For a year he refused the tiara. Finally, on May 9, 1087, he was consecrated with the name of Victor III. But on September 16, 1087, Victor III died at Monte Cassino, where the advances of Henry IV and Guibert had compelled him to take refuge.

Because of the trouble stirred up by the partisans of the antipope, the Sacred College assembled at Terracina in Campania and chose a successor to Victor III on March 12, 1088. This was Eudes (or Odo, or Otto) of Châtillon-sur-Marne in Champagne, who was a member of the Lageri family. Eudes took the name of Urban II. Urban, who was born around 1040, had studied at Rheims, and he had intended to remain there. In 1064 he had been named archdeacon of the Church of Rheims and before long a canon of the cathedral. Between 1073 and 1077 he had left Rheims to enter Cluny. So, Eudes had spent some twenty years at Rheims, first as a student of master Bruno, then as his confrère in the cathedral chapter before, like him, consecrating himself to God in the monastic life. Their meeting and their relationship will have very important consequences for Bruno's future and that of Chartreuse.

From the time of his election Urban II determined to surround himself with trustworthy men, whose perfect fidelity to the Church and to the work undertaken by Gregory VII he knew, and to involve them in the government of the Church. The first one he invited to come to see him was Hugh, the abbot of Cluny. His letter is impressive, and no official document better shows us the state of the Church than this disclosure of Urban II to his father in the monastic life. This is what he wrote:

> It was not because of ambition or a desire for dignity that I accepted my election. . . . But, in the present circumstances, if I had not brought all my support to the aid of the Church when she was in danger (*periclitanti Ecclesiæ*), I would have been afraid of offending God. . . . I entreat you, whom I wish so much to see again, if you have any affection for me, if you remember your son, your child, come to console me by your presence because I want it so much, and come to visit your holy Mother the Church of Rome, if it is possible for you, because your coming is very much desired. If it is

> not possible, at least send a delegate from among your sons, my brothers, in whom I may see you, receive you, recognize the voice of your consolation in the extremely troubling situation I find myself in; send one who will make your love and the warmth of your affection present to me, who will be a sign of kindness toward me from you and all the brothers of our congregation. Please tell all our brothers to pray to the all-powerful and merciful God until he is pleased to restore to their original condition both us and his holy Church, which is being attacked by so many dangers.

Hugh of Cluny responded to the summons of his son. Urban did not uproot him from his monastic responsibilities, but he soon took the monk John from Monte Cassino and made him cardinal-bishop of Tuscany and chancellor of holy Church. During his pontificate he called fifteen monks to the purple and authority of cardinals. In 1096 there were Albert, monk of Saint Savin of Plaisance; and Milo, monk of Saint Aubin of Angers, and others. In these choices, however, Urban II seems to have followed a rule of prudence: not usually to take from religious orders the abbot, the head, the one who encouraged them in zeal and the Rule. So when, by a letter from Capua dated August 1, 1089, he summoned Anselm, abbot of Bec, he asked him to bring along "a religious of your abbey, if there is one who can be useful to the sovereign Pontiff". He added that a student from Rome who had become a monk of Bec should be sent back to Rome "before Lent next year". Anselm himself returned to Bec.[1] That attitude may partly explain Urban II's later relationship with Bruno.

One day Bruno learned in an unexpected way that he too

[1] However, after 1097 he ordered Bernard, Abbot general of Vallombrosa, under pain of ecclesiastical censures, to rejoin him at Rome and soon made him cardinal-priest.

had been summoned to Rome by the Pope, not just to be there for a time but to live there. In its concise style the Chronicle *Magister* relates the event clearly: "Master Bruno, . . . having left the world, founded the wilderness of Chartreuse and governed it for six years. On the formal order (*cogente*) of Pope Urban, whose master he had been, he came to the Roman Curia as an aide to the Pope, to be a spiritual light for him and his counsellor in the affairs of the Church."

When and how did Urban II's order reach Bruno? To set a date for that there are only two points of reference from the Chronicle *Magister*: Bruno stayed "in Chartreuse for six years", and he died "about eleven years after he left Chartreuse". Even with these two facts, the missing date remains unclear, but "six years after Bruno arrived at Chartreuse" and "eleven years before he died" would be somewhere between the last months of 1089 and the first months of 1090.

Of course, historians try to be exact, and so they would prefer the one that coincides with events that are certain. Urban II had several times called important people to him so he could receive their advice. In May of 1089, Renaud du Bellay, archbishop of Rheims, left for Rome at the Pope's invitation. He had been named to the See of Rheims after Bruno refused it.[2] Now he stayed with the Pope for some time. He participated in the Council of Melfi in 1089, and on December 25 of the same year he received important privileges from the Pope in the form of the *pallium*, the primacy of the ecclesiastical province of lower Belgium, and confirmation for the See of Rheims with the right to conse-

[2] Between Manassès I and Renaud du Bellay, Hélinand, bishop of Laon, "purchased" the See of Rheims and was there for a short time.

crate the kings of France. After Christmas Renaud returned to his diocese. Would he have been the one commissioned to give Bruno the order to go to Rome? He must have discussed Bruno with Urban II. Between these two men, who had talked about the condition of the Church of France, the reforms to be introduced, and especially the holy and courageous men to be found and placed at the disposition of the lawful Pope, how could the name of Bruno have failed to come up, as well as the foundation of Chartreuse, and the important spiritual position of the hermitage? Both of them had studied under Bruno and still had vivid memories of what had happened at Rheims. The Pope and the Bishop carefully weighed this important decision, because to take Bruno away from that spiritual experience might be to condemn the promising new enterprise to death. Finally the Pope decided to take the risk. But rather than send his order through an anonymous messenger, he would have preferred to entrust it, in respect for his old teacher, to a mutual friend, who was also taking up (the Pope had confirmed it by his privilege of December 25) one of the highest ecclesiastical positions in the kingdom.

If this theory is granted, the events would have gone something like this. Renaud left Rome after Christmas and took Urban II's secret order to Bruno. This wintertime journey, across some regions filled with partisans of the antipope Guibert, would have had to take around four weeks. About the end of January 1090, Renaud would have arrived at Grenoble and given Bruno the order to leave for Rome. The concurrence of events makes this not merely a theory, but one that is likely, at least.

The unembellished phrases from the Chronicle *Magister* might make Bruno's departure seem easy. In fact, though, if Bruno's obedience to Urban II was complete and unconditional from the moment his order came, the news must have caused great confusion for the hermits among whom he lived. How could they imagine the wilderness of Chartreuse without the presence of the one who was the soul of it? They decided to end their experience and disband. At that time there were many hermitages; sometimes hermits left their solitude and returned to their former way of life, or the group joined some neighboring abbey. Bruno tried in vain to prevent that act of desperation. But they made their decision. They separated.

That this dispersion occurred is demonstrated by a letter of Urban II and by the legal deed of Seguin (of whom more below). It is also certain that there was some urgency to abandon the Chartreuse.

There was need to hurry because, since his companions had decided not to continue the Chartreuse experience without him, Bruno had to make arrangements about the property before he left. In agreement with Bishop Hugh of Grenoble, in whose jurisdiction lay the lands of Chartreuse, it was decided to return the area to the abbey of Chaise-Dieu, in the person of its abbot, Seguin. Seguin was one of the donors—the only ecclesiastical one—in the document of 1086. It was normal for monastic property to revert to a monastery. Besides, the priory of Mont Cornillon, located at the entry to the mountains of Chartreuse, was a dependency of Chaise-Dieu, so this priory would be the obvious one to receive the property of the hermitage. Bruno drew up the act of donation. Renaud had to return to Chaise-Dieu, some twenty miles north of Puy. He wanted to ask that famous, devout abbey to send some monks to the abbey of Saint Nicaise at Rheims, because it was in need of reform. Hugh of Grenoble accompanied Renaud to preside personally over the committee that ratified the gift of the Chartreuse, which

Bruno made over to Seguin. Bruno may have traveled with them, as well as William, abbot of Saint-Chaffre.[3]

This moment of Bruno's life is perhaps the one that best displays his spiritual greatness. For him it meant giving up that for which he had given up everything and receiving again everything he had renounced for it. The solitude of Chartreuse, which he had acquired at the cost of so much persistence, patience, and renunciation and in which he had finally found the deepest inspiration for his soul—namely, the pure love of God, this spiritual experience that seemed in every way to be favored by God and producing wonderful fruits of holiness—all this, upon a command of the Pope, suddenly came to nothing. Now he had to go to the Roman court, where he again found, worse than before, all the cares, all the dangers, all that intrigue that he had escaped when he left Rheims. If only his friends, his companions, had agreed to continue the experience or at least to try to continue. But no. If he went, they would go. This, too, was part of his sacrifice. Even in their brave effort to be detached from the world, that the little group had kept their affection for him too warm was for Bruno surely an

[3] Conveniently, the Carthusian Fathers' study that we are following mentions other theories that would equally correspond to the definite dates that we have for the historical documents; e.g., it was not with Renaud of Rheims but with William, the abbot of Saint Chaffre, a friend of Hugh of Grenoble and of Bruno, that Urban II would have discussed calling Bruno. William traveled to Rome in April 1090. His call would have arrived at Chartreuse in May 1090, and Bruno would have left in June. "Therefore, the 'six years' would correspond exactly." The letter, by which the Pope required Seguin to restore the Chartreuse properties to Bruno's companions (more about that will follow), would have been written in July, received in August, and executed within thirty days, according to the desire of Urban II, on September 17, 1090. We prefer the theory that we advanced, because it seems to satisfy many details better. In any case, between the two theories there is a difference of only six months.

occasion of humiliation rather than consolation. Now more than sixty years old, he was faced with totally giving up his original plan, for which he had struggled so much. The hermitage of Chartreuse—that "child" of his love for God, that reality that he had conceived, formed, built, and organized to offer to God as a sacrifice of praise—was destroyed by a command of the Church, a command of one of his old students who had become Pope.

In the lives of many saints, especially in the lives of saints who have created something for the glory of God, an hour comes when God requires them, in an act of obedience or faith (essentially they are the same), to sacrifice their work. A poignant hour, a sorrowful one, but it is the supreme hour in which the soul, if it consents, is compelled to strive for the summit in faith, hope, and charity. Nothing remains for it except God, to be apprehended in his transcendence, in his absolute independence, to be loved simply because he is God. One such sacrifice was that of Abraham sacrificing Isaac, the son of the Promise, with his own hands. The comparison is accurate. At the moment of obedience, Bruno must have been aware that he had created something great for God, a kind of life that held real promise for the reform of the Church, and that his departure from Chartreuse would bring it to an end.

But then the companions who had gone their ways began to think better of it. Reflecting on Bruno's counsel, they began to doubt the wisdom of their decision. They got in touch with each other and then had a meeting with Bruno, who might have been waiting in the neighborhood of Chartreuse until Hugh of Grenoble came back to Chaise-Dieu, or he might have accompanied him there to visit Seguin. Bruno and his sons then reconsidered the situation. He gave the same advice, counseling them to stay at Chartreuse and continue their spiritual experience together. He would be loyal to them from Rome and help them with his advice and friendship. And then, who could know? Perhaps some day circumstances would change again, and he could return.

They reversed their decision. Accepting Bruno's advice, the community came together again, and he named Landuino their new prior. But there was one serious problem: the hermits no longer had possession of the Chartreuse. They had to regain that before they could resume their life, because they needed it to assure their subsistence and independence. So Bruno asked Seguin to give them the lands again. This was a step that caused him some humiliation. Even though his own stability was beyond question, their coming back could be an indication to people who did not understand their internal life very well that there was some instability among the hermits as well as real uncertainty about the future of the foundation.

According to the above hypothesis Bruno left for Rome in February of 1090, accompanied no doubt by his friend William, abbot of the monastery of Saint-Chaffre, who was also going to Rome on abbey business. During the trip he was worrying about serious problems. Would the group persevere, now that they had come together again through his desire and encouragement? Would Landuino rise to his position as prior? Would Chaise-Dieu accept the request to return the property? Uncertainty about his own future was no less painful, though he had already decided to ask Urban II for permission to return to Chartreuse, or at least to solitude, as soon as he could. He had also decided that, whatever his future would be, he would create a solitude for himself in his new life and live in the papal court as much like a hermit as he could. But what if the Pope insisted on making him a bishop or even a cardinal, as he had already done for others? While the Church was having such problems, would he have the right to abandon her? In short, he was leaving something precious but fragile behind him, and before him the horizon was completely unclear. After six years of peace, silence, and friendship in Chartreuse, these uncertainties must have weighed heavily on Bruno's heart.

He would have reached Rome in March of 1090. That must have been the time, if he traveled with William of Saint-Chaffre, because the privilege that William came to ask for was granted on April 1, 1090. Then, too, there is the curious coincidence that a broad privilege confirming all the rights and privileges of the Church of Grenoble bears the same date. Were Bruno and William ambassadors for Hugh of Grenoble in this?

So then, in the spring of 1090 Bruno arrived at the Roman court. Before following him into the new events, a word about the request addressed to Seguin concerning the recovery of the property at Chartreuse. Things seem to have gone less rapidly than Bruno had hoped.[4] Did Seguin, and perhaps even Hugh of Grenoble, not want to spend time drawing up a new legal deed to transfer the property of Chartreuse? Bruno thought it prudent to have Urban II intervene in the matter. One day—unfortunately the date is not known, but it was between March and April of 1090—the Pope wrote this letter to Seguin:

[4] In this study we shall not express any opinion about the Bull of Urban II, cited by Bligny in *Recueil des Actes* (Acte I, pp. 3–11), by which the Pope asked Archbishop Hugh of Lyons and Bishop Hugh of Grenoble to see to it that Seguin returned the wilderness of Chartreuse to Bruno's brethren. According to that Bull, Seguin's sons had already occupied the hermitage. We prefer the opinion of those who reject the authenticity of that document. Its vocabulary belongs to the Renaissance.

Urban, Bishop, servant of the servants of God, to Our very dear son Seguin, abbot of Chaise-Dieu, and to his whole monastery, greetings and apostolic benediction.

The Roman Church should come to the aid of those who work tirelessly in obedience and lighten their cares. We have called Our very dear son Bruno to serve the Apostolic See. Since he has come to Us, we cannot—because we should not—permit his hermitage to suffer any harm. So, We ask your charity, and in asking it We instruct you to establish the hermitage again with its former condition. As regards the deed of donation, which Our son Bruno wrote with his own hand returning the property to you while his brethren were dispersed, return it as you love Us so that they can be established again in their former freedom. The brethren who were dispersed are together again under the inspiration of God, and they want nothing except to persevere in their vocation in the same place. For the respect which you owe to Our directives, do not delay beyond thirty days of receiving this letter to restore the above-mentioned deed.

Urban II's letter went beyond the scope of a simple transfer of the right of ownership. It constituted the first papal approval of Chartreuse, and it affirmed one point that Bruno thought essential to his plan: the hermits' complete independence of any patronage whatever, whether from a bishop, an abbey, or a prince.

What did Seguin do? A passage from the Chronicle *Laudemus*, a document issued by the Carthusian Order, testifies to his prompt and careful obedience. "Having received the directive from Rome, Abbot Seguin willingly and joyfully obeys. To Master Landuino and his companions, he surrenders all his rights and all his authority over the property of Chartreuse."

The original deed of restoration is still preserved in the

archives of Isère. It is dated September 15, 1090. Here is the original text:

> I, Brother Seguin, Abbot of Chaise-Dieu, make known to all for now and for the future that, when Brother Bruno was called to Rome by Pope Urban and he saw the property of Chartreuse being abandoned because his brethren were leaving it, he gave the property to us and to our monastery. But now, to respond to the request of our father, Pope Urban, and made aware as we were by a report from Bruno that he, their prior, had strongly encouraged his brethren to remain in that place, I, Brother Seguin, abbot of Chaise-Dieu and with the agreement of our monks, have returned to Brother Landuino, whom Master Bruno as he was leaving named prior of the other brothers, and to all the brethren who live under his authority, the gift that Bruno had made to us in our Chapter, in the presence of the chapter members that we assembled, Bishop Hugh of Grenoble presiding. In favor of them and their successors I relinquish all authority over the property of Chartreuse so that they may use it as they wish, and to them I cede all my rights. As regards the deed that Bruno had drawn up for us, if it has not been returned to them it is because the brethren present in our Chapter have not been able to find it. But it is agreed that if this document is ever found, it belongs to them by right.
>
> In the year of the Incarnation of our Lord 1090, on the fifteenth of the calends of October, I, Brother Seguin, Abbot of Chaise-Dieu, sign this document and affix my seal, Archbishop Hugh of Lyons present and presiding.[5]

[5] That Hugh of Lyons was present and presiding in the Chapter would be surprising. But apparently the Archbishop of Lyons was taking the place of Hugh of Grenoble, who was to have been there. The latter was probably impeded, and instead of asking his metropolitan, the Archbishop of Vienne, with whom he was having some difficulties, to be his substitute, he asked the Archbishop of Lyons, who, in his capacity of primate of the Gauls, had

It was necessary to quote Urban II's letter and Seguin's deed because the typical official or legal forms seem to indicate a certain uneasiness. In other words, perhaps his friends judged Bruno's grant of the property of Chartreuse at the time the brothers left as too hasty, too radical, even perhaps somewhat imprudent. And Seguin apparently temporized —which wasn't necessarily the bad humor of a frustrated landowner, but simply the patience of an administrator— in returning what had so recently been given to him. To justify his intervention, Urban II mentioned that he had summoned Bruno and assumed some responsibility for the deed of relinquishment with an apology for the haste. Twice Seguin stressed that Bruno's gift to him was perfectly proper, as if he wanted to make allowance for the future, in case the hermitage would again cease to exist some day. And did one of the monks of the Chapter come to reclaim that recent act of relinquishment? The whole scenario exhibited uncertainty and hesitation. Apparently Seguin was acceding less to Bruno's request than to Urban's formal directive and, while obeying, prepared for the future: if their master did not come back some day, wouldn't this group of hermits either cease to exist or ask, like so many others, to be affiliated with the powerful neighboring abbey?

In September 1090, therefore, the hermitage of Chartreuse was restored to its original condition. Bruno was far away, but he was not absent. Within ten years the Chartreuse would be a testimony to the fervor and unity of his sons, the faithfulness of Landuino, and the power of Bruno's own invisible presence.

What happened to Bruno during the several weeks he

---

a kind of honorary precedence in the four ecclesiastical provinces called "the provinces of Lyons".

had been in Rome? He found Urban engaged in a very confusing and very precarious political situation. The Pope had made his solemn entry into Rome on June 30, 1089, but in the spring of 1090 the partisans of the German Emperor Henry IV and the antipope Guibert had taken the offensive against Rome, and toward the end of July 1090, Urban II was again obliged to leave the city. Where could he find refuge? The lawful Pope had only two faithful supporters in Italy. In Tuscany there was the courageous Countess Mathilda, who was, wrote Guigo, "in appearance a woman, with the soul of a man";[6] also in the southern part of the peninsula were the Norman princes, who had carved out a realm for themselves there. The Pope decided to go south. There he remained for three years. In September 1090, Bruno was in the south of Italy along with the Roman court, in that territory ruled by the Norman princes.

What were his thoughts? The Chronicle *Magister* gives us valuable information about that in a few words—as usual, too few:

> Bruno set out for the Roman court. . . . But, being unable to endure the commotion (*strepitus*) and style of life (*mores*) in the court and still very much in love with his former solitude and peace, he left it. Apparently he had even refused the archbishopric of Reggio, for which he had been chosen upon the personal wish of the Pope. Instead, he went to the wilderness of Calabria that is called La Torre.

The Chronicle *Laudemus* says that he departed "shortly after he arrived".[7]

Bruno seems to have made a loyal effort to resign himself to the rhythm of life in the papal court. It is true that cir-

[6] *Life of Saint Hugh*, PL 153, 767.

[7] The dates of the Chronicle *Laudemus* would be between 1250 and 1300.

cumstances were hardly favorable for him to return there. The difficulties of diplomacy during that time, the war, the schism, the intrigue—that was a world in which Bruno could not fit. Besides, deep in his heart remained the desire for solitude and tranquillity, all the more fervent as the situation there was so inconsistent with it. Could anyone who for six years had tasted the peace of the Chartreuse, the prayer, the friendship, the heavenly familiarity of the hermitage have become accustomed to the commotion of the Roman court in exile during that autumn of 1090?

Bruno explained his distress to Urban II and asked to be allowed to leave the court again and return to his wilderness.

But, as it happened, Urban II had a delicate post to fill. It was the archbishopric of Reggio. According to the policy of Urban II and the Norman princes, this See and several others in the peninsula were gradually being given to Latin bishops instead of Greek ones, for the purpose of diminishing the influence of the Greeks in Italy. William, a Latin, was put in the place of Basil, the Greek archimandrite who formerly occupied the See of Reggio. But Basil was still living, and he always hoped to recover his position. Then William died. The succession proved to be very delicate, because Basil enjoyed the confidence of the Emperor of Constantinople, Alexius I Comnenus, with whom at this very time Urban II was seeking a rapprochement. In 1090 the See was still unoccupied. If Urban wanted to place a Latin bishop in the See of Reggio, he had to choose a man whose personality was such that Basil could not be offended. Wasn't Bruno just such a man? He had proven his ability, in difficult matters, to combine firmness and prudence, and zeal for the truth with moderation. Besides, his reputation had long since become known throughout the Church. For him one could step aside without being humiliated.

Urban II decided to have Bruno appointed to the See of Reggio. The exact date is known. Rayner, the Benedictine monk of La Cava,[8] who was finally named archbishop of Reggio, signed a confirmation certificate in 1091, so Bruno's nomination to the archbishopric of Reggio and his refusal must have occurred between the summer of 1090 (when he arrived at the papal court) and November of 1091. This haste is not surprising. Several times Urban II nominated bishops and even cardinals very rapidly, men he had personally summoned to be with him to serve the Holy See. He speeded up the election process by announcing his selection publicly. The electors hardly knew the candidate, but they had confidence in the Pope's choice. This was clearly what happened with Bruno: he was elected "at the will of the Pope" (*ipso Papa volente*), when the Pope formally made his choice known.

The law gave the elect the right to refuse the See that was designated for him. Bruno exercised that right firmly. For the man we know he was, this must have been a serious crisis of conscience. His faith and loyalty to the Church inclined him to serve Urban II and to be responsible for the position in which the Pope thought he would be useful. But to become archbishop of Reggio would be to involve himself permanently in the "commotion", "the style of life", and everything that was profoundly distasteful to him and

[8] This Rayner must not be confused with Rayner, bishop of Lucca, who was Bruno's pupil at Rheims and dedicated to his memory one of the *Eulogies* that have been preserved (Eulogy 3). Rayner of Reggio studied at Marmoutiers. The choice of Rayner must have been a delicate matter, because he was still only an "elect" and not an ordained archbishop when he signed the acts of the Council of Clermont in November 1095.

conflicted with his craving for solitude and interior tranquillity, which he well knew, after six years in the Chartreuse, to be his true vocation. As bishop, and soon no doubt as cardinal, he would accompany the Pope in his travels, take part in all the business and the great assizes of the Church and be closely involved in papal diplomacy.[9] All that, and no hope of ever finding a hermitage again. What a moment in Bruno's life! There must have been frank and familiar conversations between him and Urban II when Bruno revealed his soul, his desires, his attractions, and his vocation to the man whose mission and grace it was to direct his life. Though Urban could have let his appointment stand and confirmed it by imposing it upon Bruno under pain of ecclesiastical censures, he finally recognized his old master's special vocation to an unusual calling. Rayner was appointed to the See of Reggio.

That decision brought honor to Urban II and to Bruno. Both of them gave way before that mysterious, clear, genuine, irrepressible reality called a vocation from God—to

[9] As the result of a mistake made by Dom Henri Kalkar in his *De ortu et progressu* (MS) (1398), repeated and used by Dom François du Puy in his *Vita Sancti Brunonis* [Life of Saint Bruno] (1515) some historians had Bruno participating in the Councils of Melfi, Troïa in Pouille, Benevento, Plaisance, and even Clermont. This legend should be abandoned, attractive as it may be for those who regret that Bruno did not play any great role in the grand affairs of the Church. No record contains any trace of Bruno's presence at any Council of that period, not even at the Council of Bénévent, although he could have been present there, because it was held from March 28 to 31, 1091. That other legend should also be abandoned, the one that imagines that Bruno wrote the preface for the Holy Virgin and had it adopted for the Council of Plaisance. The preface is definitely several centuries earlier than the pontificate of Urban II.

There is a beautiful painting of Zurbarán, representing Urban II and Bruno, just the two of them, seated facing each other. This masterpiece of monastic painting is now at Seville.

Bruno for having the courage to go against the Pope's wish, to Urban II for giving up the services of a man whom he judged so suitable to be a helper and counsellor in his problems. The Pope's decision to free Bruno seems to partake of divine inspiration, higher than any human wisdom, higher even than the holiest friendship. Urban II, of course, had been a monk; he was even formed in the school of Saint Benedict and instructed in that mysticism that makes the soul attentive to the mystery of God and endows it with the Church's understanding of a consecrated life entirely dedicated to the adoration and the praise of God in union with Christ, who died and rose to live again. In Bruno he found that vocation pure, perfect, insistent, yearning for the absolute. From all that he could see, God was there, imposing his own designs and calling. Could this former student of Saint Benedict have failed to understand that for the good of the Church it was more important that Bruno be a hermit, undertaking and achieving his work as a contemplative, than for him to be archbishop of Reggio and a dignitary in the papal court? A few months earlier Bruno sacrificed his vocation as a hermit to the Pope's summons; today, Urban II sacrificed his summons to a higher one, and through that sacrifice the Church authenticated the supreme value of the purely contemplative life for its work of Redemption. This was one of the high points in the life of Urban and the life of Bruno.[10]

[10] At this point in Bruno's life, it is important to recall the July 8, 1924, Apostolic Constitution *Umbratilem* of Pius XI. These thoughts of Pius XI reflect those that inspired Urban II's decision: "In his infinite goodness, which never fails to provide for the needs and concerns of his Church, God chose Bruno, a man of exceptional holiness, to restore the original purity of the contemplative life. . . . Our predecessor Urban II was not skimpy in his regard and favor toward Bruno, his former master in the

Here a question comes up to which history, at the present stage of research, cannot give a positive answer. Since Urban II authorized Bruno to follow the way of pure contemplation, why did he not simply authorize him to return to Chartreuse? Why did he point him to a new foundation in Calabria? Surely Bruno would have wanted to go back to Chartreuse. He never had any plan to found a religious Order; the hermitage of Chartreuse was enough for him, where conditions of geography and climate, and his plans as well, limited the number of candidates to a few; and he wanted to take his place humbly and simply in the place where for six years he had enjoyed the solitude and peace of the wilderness. Everything was calling him back to his sons at Chartreuse. He loved them, and he knew they loved him, and he thought about how happy they would be when they heard he was returning. Besides, didn't they need him? Though he corresponded with them and firmly intended to stay in touch with them, not even the most diligent correspondence could ever be equal to his being there and living with them. But his desire to return to Chartreuse conflicted with Urban II's formal decision: he had to stay in Italy.

Some mystical reasons were ascribed to the Pope earlier when he accepted Bruno's refusal of the See of Reggio. Perhaps now, at the moment he felt the weight of the Church upon him, threatened as it was from the inside by schism and from the outside by war, Urban II would have been glad to have Bruno's hermitage near him—a high place for praying

---

schools of Rheims; and having become Sovereign Pontiff, he took as counselor that man whose eminent knowledge and great devotion he knew. . . . Those whose diligent zeal is dedicated to prayer and penance, even more than those whose work is cultivating the fields of the Lord, contribute to the progress of the Church and to the salvation of the human race."

and imploring God's protection, a high place of wisdom, of recollection, and advice, to which he would have ready access. Yielding to Bruno's vocation as a hermit, Urban II could nevertheless make that vocation an attraction in his thorny diplomacy with the Norman princes, who were not the most agreeable friends. As recently as 1083, while they were supporting Gregory VII, they sacked Rome. For them to do another about-face would not be surprising. Settling Bruno in Calabria would be an honor for them, assisting in their strategy for Latinization, and it would bind them more closely to the Holy See. All this is theorizing. Only one thing is certain: Bruno did not resume his life as a hermit with some companions at Chartreuse, but in Calabria.

That fact had considerable importance for Bruno's eremitical experience. First of all, Chartreuse itself was going to show itself so permeated with Bruno's spirit that the monks could carry out his ideals in their lives with fervor, even though he was absent. Besides, in Calabria Bruno was going to show that his experience at Chartreuse, favored as it had been by conditions and circumstances, was not restricted to that location and could be repeated elsewhere with even a small number of men who, prompted by his spirit, embraced the hermitage unreservedly. To repeat, nothing was farther from Bruno's thought than founding a religious Order; but, during the remainder of his life, there would be two hermitages, both of which in very different circumstances would accomplish his own unique plan. They would not be joined by any legal bond, but they would burn with the same flame.

When did Bruno settle in Calabria? Some say 1090, others 1091 or 1092, and some as late as 1095. The last date hardly seems likely, because there is no reason, after the matter of the archbishopric of Reggio was resolved, that

Urban II would have forced Bruno to remain in the papal court. However, it is likely that Bruno needed some time to select the exact place for his new hermitage, to settle some questions related to the new foundation, poor as it was, and gather some men with whom he would form his small community. A reasonable date for the beginning of the new hermitage would be the end of 1091 or the first months of 1092. There is no way to know exactly how much time passed between Bruno's departure from the papal court and that beginning, but he seems to have been present in the court of Urban II for about one year.[11]

[11] In the eighteenth century, the Carthusian chronicler Tromby transcribed in his *Storia* (vol. II, App. I, p. 60, no. XI, no. 1), following "an ancient manuscript of the Chartreuse of Calabria", a letter dated "from the third year of the pontificate of Urban II", by which the Pope gave Bruno the church of Saint Cyriacus at the baths of Diocletian "to live there freely in solitude with a companion". This letter is a fabrication of the seventeenth century, but, in agreement with the more reputable historians, no formal judgment on its authenticity will be made here.

VII

Calabria: Return to Solitude

The Calabrian period of Bruno's life is an obscure one for the historian not only because of the legends and the edifying embellishments added by hagiographers as in the other periods of his life but also because the history of Calabria and of Bruno's foundation were particularly eventful. When one remembers what happened to Bruno's relics during the four centuries following his death (more about that later), it can hardly be surprising that memories of his time in Calabria that could have survived have practically disappeared. There is always some loss when a religious Order gives one of its "holy places" to monks of another observance for more than three centuries. However, when a break in traditions has destroyed an entire past, usually certain documents are preserved with care: namely, the titles to properties and all the records relating to them. Most of those documents regarding the Calabria foundation disappeared after the several fires, the earthquake (February 7, 1783), the destruction and pillage during the Napoleonic wars, and many other lesser events. Those are sufficient to explain the loss. What survived destruction, in spite of all that, was kept, after the beginning of the nineteenth century, in the Great Archives of Naples, where, it was thought, they would be safe. But everything, down to the very last item, was burned during the events of 1943.[1]

Another fact contributed more than a little to obscure this history. The hermitage of Calabria was lavishly endowed by Count Roger, and that wealth later became the cause of litigation. During the second half of the eighteenth century there was a long dispute between the Carthusians, who had taken possession of the property on February 27, 1514, and the treasury of Naples. The latter, for the purpose of robbing the Carthusian Order of its property, tried to prove the deeds granted by the Norman princes were invalid. The quarrel was no help to historical objectivity, especially when one of the parties had the advantage of the power of the state. Today, however, some specialists have undertaken an impartial study of the documents of donation. They have not finished their work, but it is now certain that most of the deeds that were contested by the treasury of Naples are completely authentic.[2]

Even with all these misfortunes, the historian of Saint Bruno still has some good fortune. When, on February 27, 1514, the Carthusians regained possession of the monastery of Calabria from the Cistercians, who had occupied it since 1193, Dom Constantius de Rigetis, who was born at Bologna and professed at the Chartreuse of Montelli, was sent as rector of the revived house. A year later, when the Chartreuse of Calabria was sufficiently restored, he was appointed there as a regular prior. Now Dom Constantius could work full time, systematically gleaning the archives

[1] Fortunately, about the year 1900 the learned professor Garufi photographed the original documents that still existed.

[2] On the other hand, biographers blithely made use of the Great Charter, which relates a miracle of Saint Bruno in behalf of Count Roger during the siege of Capua, though the document is apocryphal.

of the monastery. With filial devotion, he sought out and compiled everything that referred to Bruno and the first years of the foundation. As he discovered the manuscripts, he copied them with scrupulous accuracy, described them with objectivity, and distinguished their various sources; and, if he had to interpret any passages, he indicated his theories and corrections honestly, clearly indicating his own commentaries. Constantius' work has survived in the form of two copies. One of them seems trustworthy—the one that comes from Dom Severus of Trafaglione, a Carthusian of Naples, in 1629;[3] the other, which is incomplete and much more doubtful, was recopied in the eighteenth century by Tromby in his *Storia*. A critical study of the text confirms what is already known about Dom Constantius: "He was a man of great prudence and religion, moderately well educated in human letters, known for his propriety and piety" (*vir fuit magnæ prudentiæ, et religionis, et litteris humanis mediocriter eruditus, gravitate et pietate præcipuus*): he was an honest worker, sincere, exacting, precise, very careful to be accurate. It was fortunate for the historian that Constantius undertook that research in the archives of the monastery of Calabria and that it has been preserved. The authors of *Aux sources de la vie cartusienne* write: "Without Constantius the face of Saint Bruno and the history of his foundation could never have emerged from the fog of hagiographical legend."

It was necessary to explain the difficulties that face the historian of the Calabrian period of Bruno's life, so that the certainties finally acquired may be seen at their full value and clarity. All those documents were patiently taken up again, studied, and compared by recent historians of the be-

[3] In the Library of Grenoble, under the number MS 630 bis, ms. Constantius.

ginnings of the Grande Chartreuse, and a collection of very certain facts has emerged, even though numerous items remain obscure.

What was the condition of Calabria when Bruno went there to plant his new foundation? Something was said earlier about that, but it will be useful to reconstruct the circumstances of the time. He was confronted with difficulties that were very different from those he had found at Chartreuse. There the planting of his hermitage was given extraordinary assistance by Hugh of Grenoble, who understood the plan and took it on as his own project, supporting it with all of his authority, generously advising and giving aid. But Bruno worried about nature, climate, and the location, and many of the difficulties actually assisted his plan for absolute solitude. In Calabria, it was men rather than nature that obstructed his plan. The political and religious milieu Bruno was in had great influence upon his foundation. There will be more said of that later for the better understanding of his work.

Between 1057 and 1060 two of the "Norman princes", Robert Guiscard and his younger brother Roger, in spite of their weak forces, quickly conquered Apulia and Calabria, which theoretically belonged to the Greek Empire. In 1060 Robert and Roger undertook the conquest of Sicily, where they met both Greeks and Arabs, and it took them twenty years to bring their efforts to a successful conclusion, the last battle being fought in 1091. After conferring upon himself the title of duke of Apulia, Robert ruled as suzerain over the conquered lands; and Roger, with the title of count, ruled Sicily and Calabria under the suzerainty of his brother. In 1085 the conquest of Sicily was sufficiently advanced and consolidated for Duke Robert to decide to take the war into the Greek Isles. He died on Corfu, and, on July 17, 1085, his son Roger Borsa became duke of Apulia. Duke Roger was the suzerain of his uncle, Count Roger, at the time Bruno established his hermitage in Calabria.[4]

In 1091 Count Roger completed the conquest of Sicily and began to organize his new lands. While doing this, he was revealing exceptional gifts for ruling.

He had to get different ethnic elements to coexist peacefully, though they had opposed each other up to that time: Catholic Latins, Greek Christians, and Muslims. His religious policy, however, tended to favor the Latins over the Greeks, even the Greek Catholics. So it was that certain Greek bishoprics, whether because of retirement, as at Reggio, or by normal succession, were transferred to Latins. Count Roger had the Greek monks emigrate from Calabria, where he believed they had too much power, to Sicily where they would be a counterbalance to the Islamic presence.

At the time Bruno was looking for a hermitage in Calabria, therefore, it was a place favorable—almost too favorable—for Latin monasticism. Roger had despoiled the Greek monks of their possessions in Calabria and given them to Latin monks. It can be said that the Latin monks appeared as destroyers of earlier Greek monasticism.[5]

How did the sovereign pontiffs react when faced with what might be called the Norman princes' invasion of southern Italy? It is best not to consider the political war games of our times. Actually, relations between the popes and the

[4] Though old and insufficiently critical, the principal study of this whole matter remains Chalandon's book, *Histoire de la domination normande en Italie et en Sicile*, Paris, Picard, 1907. 2 vols. It is good, whenever possible, to compare the statements in it with the work that L. R. Ménager is now doing on the history of southern Italy during the Middle Ages.

[5] On this subject, cf. L. R. Ménager, "The religious 'Byzantinization' of southern Italy (ninth–twelfth centuries) and the monastic policy of the Normans in Italy" in *Revue d'Histoire ecclésiastique*, vol. LIV (1959), no. 1.

new masters of southern Italy were not always easy. It is true, nevertheless, that at the beginning of Urban II's pontificate, when Emperor Henry IV was threatening the whole peninsula with his military expeditions, the Norman princes were faithful to the Pope. Immediately after his election in the spring of 1088, Urban II judged it possible and wise to go to the south and make contact with the Normans. When Henry IV forced him to leave Rome in the summer of 1090, he returned to the territory of the Norman princes to seek and find asylum. He stayed there for three years (1090–93).

Bruno's decision to begin the hermitage, therefore, came at a time when Urban II and Count Roger wanted to give each other clear pledges of friendship, and when the papal court was not looking with disapproval upon the policy of Latinization, which Count Roger had introduced in the monastic life in Calabria. Bruno himself had just one idea: namely, insofar as circumstances would allow, to find in Calabria, where he was obliged to settle, the solitude and peace that he had enjoyed in Chartreuse.

But where? Did Bruno think he would ever find a place in Calabria so perfect, so suitable to his idea of eremitical life as Chartreuse? Biographers have undertaken to explain, or simply to praise, Bruno's choice of the region of La Torre. Some of them relate that Urban II had put Bruno in charge of an important mission to the Norman princes. Duke Roger, aware of Bruno's plans for a hermitage, had been waiting to furnish the hermits with the perfect place they were looking for; but when, at last, Bruno did not find a place suitable for his foundation in Duke Roger's land, Count Roger offered him great benefits if he would remain in his estates. Others created a legend—a gratuitous one common in the folklore of hermits—that Count Roger, while hunting, came upon Bruno, who was praying in the forest. Still others, more serious, maintained that Bruno had lived for a while in Count Roger's court before deciding on the place. That is not unlikely, unless they want to prolong his stay there. Certainly Bruno had to make some contact with Count Roger and his court so that he could look over his lands and then, after making his decision, to arrange for the administration.

But probably things happened very simply, as things do whenever a founder looks for a place suitable for a foundation: he travels around the area where he expects to find what he wants, examines all the possibilities, then makes a choice and finally arranges to possess it. The only anecdote that might be added to that in Bruno's case is that Urban II met Count Roger in the little town of Mileto at the beginning of June 1091. No doubt Urban told him about Bruno's plan and asked him to take care of it. The wilderness of La Torre is just a few kilometers from Mileto.

Nevertheless, according to the document of confirmation that was set down by the Bishop of Squillace on December 7, 1091, it is certain that the wilderness of La Torre was granted (and very probably Bruno and his companions had settled there) before December 7, 1091.

The place where Bruno established his new hermitage was called Saint Mary of La Torre. It was a wilderness, located at an altitude of about 2,600 feet, midway between the two seas and between the towns of Stylum and Arena. The deed of donation added to this two and one half square miles of land adjoining the wilderness, including the forest, meadows, pasture land, water, mills, and all seigniorial rights. A look at a map of the area will cause surprise that Bruno preferred this small place of relative and threatened solitude to others more remote in the mountains of Calabria. Was it because of prudence, since the peace of the country was uncertain? Was it for security while living among a divided population, one part of which—the Greek element—was in fact being abused for the benefit of the other—the Latin element? Perhaps the wilderness of La Torre already included some monastic buildings erected by the Greeks. Stylum, in fact, was one of the places that supported the Greek resistance to the Normans at the time of the 1060 conquest. At any rate, Saint Mary of La Torre did not offer the same natural protections for the solitude of the hermits as the Chartreuse did. In his letter to Raoul le Verd, Bruno used a rather unenthusiastic phrase to describe his solitude: "I live in a wilderness located in Calabria, sufficiently distant (*satis remotam*) from any center of human habitation." Comparing it to the location of the Chartreuse would have strengthened his description.

When he left for Saint Mary of La Torre, Bruno did not go alone. He had companions, just as he did when he went up to Chartreuse. Who were they, and where did they come from? In the letter to Raoul le Verd, he said he was living "with my brothers in religion, some of whom are filled with knowledge", which shows that the group had attained a certain number of hermits. The letter dates, at the earliest, from 1096, and at that time the small community must have numbered fifteen to twenty members. When Saint Bruno died, there were thirty. Thanks to Constantius, there are two lists of Bruno's companions in Calabria: one is a necrology[6] of the foundation (which also contains the profession of faith that Bruno made before he died), and the list of thirty hermits who took their oath to blessed Lanuino in 1101. None of the names of the first six companions from Chartreuse appear in it, though that does not absolutely exclude the

[6] That is, a list of the names of the dead, with the day of their death or burial, etc.

possibility that some of the hermits from Chartreuse had accompanied Bruno or joined him in Italy.[7] It appears that Lanuino was one of the first of Bruno's companions in Calabria: he was a Norman, a Norman who was very skillful in business, as will be observed. But was this Norman among the noblemen? Did he come from Chartreuse with Bruno? Did he come from France when he found out that Bruno was going to found a new hermitage? Perhaps what happened was very simple: when Bruno's plan became known, given his buoyant personality and the attraction that many

[7] We prefer to leave the question open, though personally we tend to favor a negative answer. Two lists seem to indicate that some hermits, including Lanuino, came from Chartreuse with Bruno.

First there is the charter of donation from Count Roger (1090): "We want to let you know that, by the mercy of God, some men named Bruno and Lanuino, full of enthusiasm for religion, have come to our land of Calabria from France with some companions. Despising all the vanities of the world, they have determined to live for God alone. Knowing their holy desire and wishing to share in their prayers, we have—with considerable effort—brought it about that they have chosen a place in our lands that is suitable to serve God according to their desire."

The other charter comes from Duke Roger, who in 1094 confirmed the donation of Count Roger: "Bruno and Lanuino have come to Calabria from France with their companions. They are enthusiastic with holy zeal and admirable piety. God has surely willed for them to come into our duchy; but, because they could not find a sufficiently solitary place among our lands, Roger, count of Calabria and Sicily, has received them in his territory."

Unfortunately both of these charters seem to be spurious. They are not among the items relating to the privileges of the churches of his fief that Roger II, son of Count Roger, an excellent administrator, assembled in 1144.

Two other items are also missing: the great charter of the narration of the apparition of Bruno to Count Roger during the siege of Capua and the list of traitors from the siege of Capua who were handed over to be servants at Bruno's hermitage. For various reasons we regard these items to be spurious.

felt for the eremitical life, some of the Norman emigrés (including Lanuino) might naturally have revealed themselves to him and asked to accompany him. Seemingly there were both laymen and clerics among them, as at the foundation of Chartreuse. The Chronicle *Magister*, which did not waste words, tells about the foundation of the house at Calabria in this fashion: "Bruno . . . withdrew to the wilderness of Calabria, which is called La Torre, and there, with several (*quamplurimis*) laymen and clerics, he led the solitary life, according to his plan, just as he had done before."

The central fact, which is well established, is that before the end of 1091 Bruno had founded the new hermitage of Saint Mary of La Torre, and he was living there with several companions, both laymen and clerics. He lived there for ten years.

Consequently the historian faces an important question that concerns not just the Carthusian Order but anyone who has followed the development of Bruno's rare, unqualified attraction for solitude with God. On account of the doubt about the authenticity of the documents of the donations in Calabria,[8] papal documents, and civil deeds as well, it can be maintained—depending upon two documents, one of 1098 or 1099 (the famous document that had been delivered by Count Roger when he returned from the siege of Capua), and the other of June 4, 1102 (concerning the traitors from the siege of Capua)—the group of monks that Bruno had himself established in Calabria were somewhat different from those at Chartreuse. There were two houses one mile apart: the true and strict hermitage of Saint Mary of La Torre, and a place called Saint Stephen, which might

[8] These are the legal deeds in which are recorded donations of lands, dwellings, farms, and even serfs and in general every grant of rights. Cf. below, pp. 165–67.

also have been a hermitage but more probably had been a monastery of cenobites for the religious who were not suited for the eremitical life and for novices to receive their first formation. If so, Bruno's original plan for absolute purity, for a complete contemplative life, had been greatly modified. He would have come closer to some of the communities combining hermitage and cenobium that already existed in the Church, like the Camaldolese. Bruno himself would then be responsible for the rapid evolution of Saint Mary of La Torre, because the cenobium (which was actually founded twenty years after Bruno's death) developed to the detriment of the hermitage, so much so that in 1193 William of Messina asked that the Chartreuse of Calabria be received into the Cistercian Order.

Recent research by the Carthusian Fathers has definitely established that the two documents were spurious and that there was never a cenobium at Saint Mary of La Torre during Bruno's time. The house of Saint Stephen was not founded until twenty years after Bruno's death. Meanwhile, in 1114, the monastery of Saint James had been founded at the village (*casale*) of Montauro, having a church dedicated to Saint James, where Count Roger had given a large area to the hermits of Saint Mary of La Torre in 1094. At the request of Lanuino, the second master of the wilderness, the Pope erected a monastery there, which was intended for religious who found the strict rule of the hermitage had become too difficult, as well as for the old and the sick. There, too, candidates for the eremitical life were to spend one year of probation before being admitted to Saint Mary. This foundation originated thirteen years after Bruno's death. But it does not present the same problems as Saint Stephen: Saint James of Montauro is located near the town of Squillace on the Ionian Sea, twenty-five miles from Saint Mary of

La Torre, so there could have been no confusion possible between the hermitage of Saint Mary and the cenobium of Saint James.

One important fact emerges from those studies: while Bruno was living, the only institution that existed in the wilderness of La Torre was Saint Mary, and it was a hermitage.

Now that this point of history has been clarified, the way is open again to recreate the milieu in which Bruno lived and led his companions to live at Saint Mary of La Torre. Everything comes together to provide a glimpse of Bruno's perfect loyalty to himself and to the grace of a purely contemplative life. The documents, both papal and episcopal, reveal the admiration and esteem that Bruno enjoyed: his extraordinary goodness, which is legendary; his sensitive and solid friendships; his great devotion; his love of solitude and peace; his human and spiritual enthusiasm among his brethren and contemporaries, especially the papal court and Count Roger. Even making allowances for the inevitable exaggeration that is typical of such documents, the man who was the object of so much reverence, respect, and affection was certainly an exceptionally religious person, and his ideal of a life entirely consecrated to loving God and to pure contemplation awakened a profound echo in the soul of those who came into contact with him.

VIII

The Contemplative Life in Bruno's Letters

Much more valuable and certain than all the testimonials from Bruno's friends are the two letters that he wrote during his years in Calabria recounting conditions as they were then, one to his friend Raoul le Verd, and the other to the brethren at Chartreuse. Both of them belong to his last years. The letter to Raoul le Verd was written between 1096 and 1101, and the other in 1099 or 1100. In each of them Bruno speaks freely and clearly. With Raoul he uses a more literary, polished style, showing some erudition; with his brethren at Chartreuse he speaks simply, using plain, warm language. Both of them show touching sincerity and openness, revealing the depth of his soul in a wonderful light that is distinct yet subdued, near the end of his life, at the conclusion of his experience in pure contemplation.

This study of Bruno's soul should include the profession of faith that he wanted to make before he died (more about that below). His emphasis and his expressions provide an earlier insight into his inner life.

First, the letter to Raoul le Verd. Raoul was one of the two friends Bruno met with in Adam's garden when they made the vow to leave the world and embrace monastic life. Years had passed since then. Bruno had fulfilled his vow; Raoul returned to Rheims and stayed there. When the provost Manassès became archbishop of Rheims in 1096, Raoul was named provost of the cathedral Chapter, but the friendship between Bruno and Raoul did not wane. Bruno tells us that Raoul wrote "warm letters, in which he tactfully reaffirms his friendship", "he lavishes his favors" to Bruno and Brother Bernard, he gives "still more testimonials" of "his affection". Bruno answered his letters. But from their correspondence nothing now exists except this important letter.

Bruno regarded God as the source of friendship. He was troubled about the spiritual future of his friend, because Raoul had made a clear, formal vow, and he did not fulfill it. He was not right with God. What would happen to him in eternity if he died in perjury? "If you should leave this life—may God preserve you!—before fulfilling the obligation of your vow, you will leave me destroyed by sadness and without hope for consolation." Then, very strongly, sometimes severely, but always tactfully, Bruno explained to Raoul the seriousness of his position. Before any commentary, the letter should be read here:[1]

1. Bruno, to the esteemed Lord Raoul, provost of the Chapter of Rheims: health in the spirit of true charity.

I am aware of your loyalty to our long and constant friendship, the more wonderful and excellent as it is found so rarely among men. Great distances and many years have separated us, but they have not diminished your affection for your friend. By your warm letters and your many kindnesses to

[1] This letter is a translation of a twelfth-century manuscript, which came from the Abbey of Saint-Arnoul in Metz, now kept in the National Library of Berlin (Berlin. Natl. Lib. Philipps 1694 [Cat. rose 180] fol. 27, vº 29).

me, and to Brother Bernard for my sake, you have reassured me of your friendship, and in many other ways besides. For your goodness, I send thanks. Though they are less than you deserve, they come from a love that is pure.

2. A long time ago I sent a messenger with some letters to you. He was faithful on other errands, but this time he has not come back. So I thought about sending one of our monks to explain my concerns in person, because I cannot do it adequately by letter.

3. Now I want you to know—hoping it will not displease you—that I am in good health and things are going as well as I could wish. I pray God that it is the same for my soul. In my prayer I await the divine mercy to heal my inner weakness and grant the blessings I desire.

4. I am living in a wilderness in Calabria, sufficiently distant from any center of human population. I am with my religious brethren, some of whom are very learned. They persevere in their holy life, waiting for the return of the master, ready to open the door for him as soon as he knocks. How can I speak adequately about this solitude, its agreeable location, its healthful and temperate climate? It is in a wide, pleasant plain between the mountains, with verdant meadows and pasturelands adorned with flowers. How can I describe the appearance of the gently rolling hills all around, and the secret of the shaded valleys where so many rivers flow, the brooks, and the springs? There are watered gardens and many fruit trees of various kinds.

5. But why am I giving so much time to these pleasantries? For a wise man there are other attractions, which are still more pleasant and useful, being divine. Nevertheless, scenes like these are often a relaxation and a diversion for fragile spirits wearied by a strict rule and attention to spiritual things. If the bow is stretched for too long, it becomes slack and unfit for its purpose.

6. Only those who have experienced the solitude and si-

lence of the wilderness can know what benefit and divine joy they bring to those who love them.

There strong men can be recollected as often as they wish, abide within themselves, carefully cultivate the seeds of virtue, and be nourished happily by the fruits of paradise. There one can try to come to clear vision of the divine Spouse who has been wounded by love, to a pure vision that permits them to see God. There they can dedicate themselves to leisure that is occupied and activity that is tranquil. There, for their labor in the contest, God gives his athletes the reward they desire: a peace that the world does not know and joy in the Holy Spirit.

Remember lovely Rachel. Although she gave Jacob fewer offspring than Leah, he preferred her to the more fruitful one, whose vision was dim. The offspring of contemplation are more rare than the offspring of action; so it was that their father had more affection for Joseph and Benjamin than for their other brothers.

Remember that better part, which Mary chose and which would not be taken away from her.

7. Remember the lovely Sunamitess, that virgin who was the only one in the land of Israel found worthy to attend to David and warm him when he was old. I should like for you, too, dear brother, to love God above all, so that warmed by his embrace you may be aflame with divine love. May this charity take root in your heart so that the glory of the world, that captivating and deceptive temptation, will soon seem abhorrent to you; that you will reject the riches whose cares are a burden to the soul; and that you will find those pleasures, so harmful to body as well as spirit, distasteful.

8. You should always be aware of the one who wrote these words: "If anyone loves the world and what is in the world —the concupiscence of the flesh, the covetousness of the eyes and pride—the love of the Father is not in him"; and

these, too: "Whoever wishes to be a friend of this world becomes an enemy of God." Is there any greater sin, any worse folly and downfall of the spirit, anything more hurtful or unfortunate, than to wish to be at war against the one whose power cannot be resisted and whose just vengeance cannot be evaded? Are we stronger than he? If, for the moment, his patient goodness moves us to repentance, will he not at last punish the offenses of those who disregard him? What is more perverse, more contrary to reason, to justice, and to nature itself, than to prefer creature to Creator, to pursue perishable goods instead of eternal ones, those of earth rather than those of heaven?

9. My dear friend, what do you intend to do? What, if not to believe God's counsels, to believe Truth who cannot deceive? This is his counsel to you: "Come to me, you who are heavily burdened, and I will refresh you." Isn't it a burden both unprofitable and unproductive to be tormented by concupiscence, constantly under attack by the cares, anxieties, fears, and sorrows that are the result of those desires? What heavier burden is there than that which makes the soul descend from its sublime dignity down to the underworld, where all holiness is held in contempt? Then, my brother, flee all this agitation and misery, and go from the storm of this world to the cove where there is tranquil and certain rest.

10. You know what Wisdom herself says to us: "If you do not renounce all your possessions, you cannot be my disciple." Is there anyone who cannot see how beautiful and useful and pleasant it is to dwell in his school under the guidance of the Holy Spirit, there to learn divine philosophy, which alone can confer true happiness?

11. So, it is important for you to consider your duty carefully. If the invitation from love does not suffice for you, if the glimpse of useful goods does not impel you, at least let necessity and the fear of punishment restrain you.

12. You know the promise you made and to whom you made it. He is all-powerful and terrible, that Lord to whom you consecrated yourself in a pleasing oblation. It is not permitted to lie to him, nor is it profitable, because he does not permit himself to be mocked with impunity.

13. You will remember that day when we were together —you, Fulco le Borgne, and I—in the little garden beside Adam's house, where I was staying. We talked for some time, I think, about the false attractions and the perishable riches of this world and about the joys of eternal glory. With fervent love for God we then promised, we vowed, we decided soon to leave the shadows of the world to go in search of the good that is everlasting and receive the monastic habit. We would have carried out our plan had Fulco not gone to Rome, but we put it off until he would return. He delayed, and other matters came up, his courage waned, and his enthusiasm cooled.

14. What else is there for you to do, my dear friend, but to acquit yourself of this pledge as soon as possible? Otherwise you will have been guilty of a lie all this time, and you will incur the wrath of the all-powerful One as well as the terrible sufferings to come. What sovereign would permit one of his subjects to deny him with impunity a service that had been promised, particularly a service he valued highly? Do not take my word for it, but believe the prophet and the Holy Spirit saying: "Make vows to the Lord, your God, and fulfill them; let all round about him bring gifts to the terrible Lord who checks the pride of princes, who is terrible to the kings of the earth" (Ps 76:12f). Pay attention: this is the voice of the Lord, the voice of your God, the voice of the one who is terrible and who checks the pride of princes, the voice of the one who is terrible to other kings of the earth. Why does the Spirit of God teach that so strongly, if not to encourage you earnestly to do what you promised by your vow? Why is it hard for you to fulfill a vow that will not cause you to lose

nor even diminish anything you have but will rather bring you great profit from the one to whom you owe it?

15. Do not allow yourself to be delayed by deceitful riches —they cannot relieve our poverty; nor by the dignity of the provost's office—it cannot be exercised without great peril to the soul. Permit me to say that it would be repugnant and unjust to appropriate for your own use the possessions of which you are merely the administrator, not the owner. If the desire for honor and glory inclines you to live in style— and you cannot afford those expenses on what you possess —do you not in one way or another deprive some people of what you give to others? That is not an act of beneficence or of generosity. No act is charitable if it is not just.

16. But I would like to discourage you from withdrawing from divine charity in favor of serving the Archbishop, who trusts your advice and depends upon it. It is not easy to give sound, beneficial advice all the time. Divine love, being more sound, is more beneficial. What is more sound and more beneficial, more innate, more in accord with human nature than to love the good? And what is as good as God? Still more, is there anything good besides God? So, the holy soul who has any comprehension of this good, of his incomparable brilliance, splendor, and beauty, burns with the flame of heavenly love and cries out: "I thirst for God, the living God. When will I come and see the face of God?" (Ps 42:3).

17. My brother, do not disregard this admonition from your friend. Do not turn a deaf ear to the words of the Holy Spirit. Rather, my dearest friend, satisfy my desire and my long waiting, so that my worry, anxiety, and fear for you will torment me no longer. If you should leave this life—may God preserve you!—before having fulfilled what you owe by your vow, you would leave me destroyed by sadness and without hope for consolation.

18. That is why I beg you to grant my wish: at least come

on a devotional pilgrimage to Saint Nicholas, and from there to me. You will see the one who loves you more than anyone else, and together we will talk about our affairs, our religious observance, and what concerns the good of us both. I trust in the Lord that you will not regret having undertaken the difficulty of such an arduous journey.

19. I have exceeded the bounds of an ordinary letter because, being unable to enjoy having you here, I wanted to talk with you a little longer by writing this.

I sincerely hope that you, my brother, will long remain in good health and remember my advice.

Please send me *The Life of Saint Remi*, because it is impossible to find a copy where we are.

Farewell.

There is the wonderful letter. It seems to have been intended primarily to persuade Raoul to fulfill his old vow as soon as possible. Commentators have not failed to recognize an unusual development in Bruno's argument. The reasoning proceeds symmetrically; it is, as it were, "wrapped up". First there is the motif of love (7); then an appeal to a higher interest (8, 9, 10); following that comes an appeal to fear (11, 12, 14); then another appeal to interest (beginning in 16); and finally again an appeal to love (16). But Bruno's letter goes beyond the affair of Raoul. It practically constitutes a short treatise on the solitary life, and that is the issue here: How did he understand the life of the wilderness, and especially how did he perceive it after having experienced it, now that he had lived it and he was living it still: "Only those who have experienced the solitude and silence of the wilderness can know what benefit and divine joy they bring to those who love them (6)."[2]

The thread of this letter is the love of God: only the love

[2] *Lettres des Premiers Chartreux*, T. I, p. 50.

of God explains and really justifies dedicating oneself to the contemplative life. And not the love of God as it is commonly lived, either, but fervent, burning love of God, an extraordinary love like that which the Holy Spirit himself once placed in the heart of the three friends when they were together in Adam's little garden: "with fervent love for God we promised, vowed" (13). Bruno several times repeated this expression in his letter, scarcely modifying it at all. Referring to "the lovely Sunamitess", a symbol of the beauty of God, he wrote: "So I should like for you, dear brother, to love him above all, so that, warmed by his embrace you may be aflame with divine love (*divino caleres amore*)." And at the conclusion of his letter, confiding to his friend his final hope, Bruno said: "And what is as good as God? Still more, is there anything good besides God? So, the holy soul who has any comprehension of this good, of his incomparable brilliance, splendor, and beauty, burns with the flame of heavenly love and cries out: 'I thirst for God, the living God. When will I come and see the face of God?' (Ps 42:3)". At the beginning of his eremitical vocation, at the heart of his contemplative experience, burns and flames that extraordinary love of God.

What is the love of God to which Bruno refers? He speaks of that love of God to which the Incarnation and redemption of Jesus Christ give us access, of that filial love that is a participation in the same love exchanged by the Divine Persons within the Trinity. The numerous references to the Holy Spirit, to his profound activity in the soul, are our guarantee of that love: "There, for their labor in the contest, God gives his athletes the reward they desire: a peace that the world does not know and joy in the Holy Spirit" (6). "Is there anyone who cannot see how beautiful and useful and pleasant it is to dwell in his school under the guidance of the Holy Spirit, there to learn divine philosophy, which alone can confer true happiness?" (10). It is the Holy Spirit who spoke to the heart of Raoul the "terrible" words that should fill him with fear for not fulfilling his vow (14). "Do not turn a deaf ear to the words of the Holy Spirit" (17). Addressing these entreaties to his friend, Bruno intended only to be the interpreter of the Holy Spirit, who was urging Raoul from within.

The essential, fundamental quality of the contemplative, according to Saint Bruno, is living expectant and hopeful with eternity always in view. Bruno describes his companions in these words: "They constantly keep a holy watch, awaiting the return of the master, so they may open for him when he knocks." In general, the life of the wilderness does not leave the soul in this place of waiting and hoping. At the moment they made their vow God granted the three friends their desire: in the solitude and silence to "capture what is lasting" while they were still here in this world.[3] "There valiant men can be recollected as much as they wish, develop their interior life, diligently cultivate the seeds of virtue, and happily produce the fruits of paradise." Striving and already possessing; desiring and already enjoying; struggling and already having the reward; in a desert that is already an orchard —this for Bruno is the call to pure contemplation. In a wonderful phrase he expresses this paradox of the contemplative state, this mystery of suffering and of joy that is the foun-

[3] *Captare* signifies, in the first place, to be on a search to take something. We might use the word *capture*, or *possess*. It was first in Adam's little garden that the three friends decided to leave everything to go in search of the treasures that will last. Those who did in fact leave everything are still on a search, and being on a search they already possess. Besides, *captare*, even in Latin, can mean *capture*. Finally, Bruno himself indicates that the contemplatives around him "feed with joy on the fruits of paradise".

dation of his existence: "There we try to acquire the clear vision that wounds our Divine Spouse with love and, clear and pure, allows us to see God." His concise Latin phrase for this should be given: *Hic oculus ille conquiritur, cujus sereno intuitu vulneratur sponsus amore, quo mundo et puro conspicitur Deus.* Speaking of one who lives in the city of the angels, Saint Augustine said: *Est, videt, amat: in æternitate Dei viget, in veritate Dei lucet, in bonitate Dei gaudet* (He is, he sees, he loves: the eternity of God is his life, the truth of God is his light, the goodness of God is his joy).[4] That is the destiny of the contemplative but, while he is in this world, this life cannot be without effort, this truth not without obscurity, this joy not without sorrow.

Sereno intuitu: here this is translated by the words "clear vision". Actually, *serenus* means more. Along with the notion of clarity, of limpidity, there is also the notion of peace, calm, repose. Here we find a notion that is very dear to Bruno, the notion of *quies*, the quiet that is central to the Carthusian concept of contemplative life. This rest is the fruit of faith, hope, and love. It prepares the way for wisdom, balance, goodness, patience, spiritual virginity. *Quietus* is his favorite word to describe "the gate of the religious life", both in the letter to Raoul le Verd and in the letter to the brethren of Chartreuse. This "quiet" is not comfort, security, immobility, passivity. Rather, it is active, dynamic. It is the anticipation of the divine rest that contemplating God will give to the soul in eternity. The first generations of Carthusians were not deceived about that: in chapter XV of the *Customs*, Guigo prescribed that the prior give his monks "an example of rest, stability, and the other practices that affect their life".

[4] Cited by *Lettres des Premiers Chartreux*, I, p. 63, n. 2.

At this point it is useful to observe that the contemplative life is a special vocation, particularly one lived in the ultimate purity that Bruno embraced. "The sons of contemplation are more rare than the sons of activity." One of the *Eulogies* recounts that a monk "who loved Bruno very much used to say that he alone of all his contemporaries had renounced the world". By the grace given to him personally and by the grace given him as founder he had the privilege to "capture what is lasting" in an outstanding degree. He really set himself, and those who wanted to follow him to that strictness of observance, at the border of two universes: the universe of God, his grace and his love, and the universe of this world, where everything, even the hierarchy and the clergy, are almost fatally spoiled by imperfection or sin. His vision cannot be comprehended except as God's call to perfect love; it is a vision that Bruno had the right to express in all its rigor, considering what he had seen, heard, and suffered at Rheims. It is a vision that he had the right, as a friend, confidant, and companion in the effort, to ask Raoul to consider. But it is a vision that cannot come to clergy or laymen whom God calls to remain "in the world but not of the world".[5]

Nevertheless, when Bruno defined the beauties and the requirements of the purely contemplative life, he did a great service for all Christians, even those living "in the world". He presented the qualities and the effects of contemplative prayer on their own level. Even if it were only stammering to begin with, silence, recollection, simplicity, and purity would come to them as a result of their sincere love for God.

[5] A propos of §16 of our letter, the author of "Letters of the first Carthusians" remarks, not without humor: "If [this] paragraph had to be taken logically, the reasoning would be faulty, because it would follow that there must be no more provosts or bishops" (p. 54, n. 1).

According to that pattern for contemplative life, to which his friend Raoul had vowed himself, as Bruno also had, that day in Adam's garden, he described what could be called the conditions for an absolute love for God.

It is a climate of spiritual energy and strength. "There strong men can be recollected as often as they wish, abide within themselves, carefully cultivate the seeds of virtue." Silence and solitude are at once conditions for contemplation and the fruits of contemplation. That spiritual strength leads the soul to be courageous in sacrificing "deceitful riches" and renouncing the honors and burdens of the world: this renunciation, generosity, and magnanimity in sacrifice, which astonish the world and sometimes the soul itself, are simply the effects of divine charity: "May this charity take root in your heart so that soon the glory of the world, that captivating and deceptive temptation, will seem abhorrent to you, and you will easily reject the riches whose cares are a burden to the soul, finding those pleasures, so harmful to body as well as spirit, distasteful." Precisely there lay the sin of Raoul, which exposed him to the wrath of God: he had been the object of a call to pure love, he possessed the grace to renounce all those things, and he procrastinated. "What is more perverse, more contrary to reason, to justice, and to nature itself, than to prefer creature to Creator, to pursue perishable goods instead of eternal ones, those of earth rather than those of heaven?" Detachment from riches and honors as well as poverty and humility are indispensable for the "strong men". Even the grace of a contemplative vocation includes a mysterious light that reveals not only that creatures are nothing and that God is everything but also the strength to be detached from them in order to be attached to God alone.

In Bruno's vision that strength of soul does not imply

tension. There is truth in the image of the bow that cannot always be taut for fear it will either grow slack or break, a traditional figure in mystical literature. After writing lyrically about the beauties of Saint Mary of La Torre, Bruno continued: "Scenes like these are a relaxation and a diversion for fragile spirits wearied by a strict rule and attention to spiritual things. If the bow is stretched too long, it becomes slack and ill suited to its purpose." Bruno's balance was legendary. In the view of many it was, along with goodness, his "specialty". But let the word not be misunderstood. Balance, according to Bruno, is not the motionlessness of the scales or some kind of alternating of contraries that cancel each other. Rather, it is the harmonious combination of two positive qualities, two pure occupations, two opposite sentiments, both of which are pleasing to God. Strength, said Bruno, must be combined with gentleness, moderation, and humility. The spiritual combat that is the labor of contemplation becomes easier by simple, reverent contact with creation. Solitude must be both energy and rest. Bruno rejoiced that his hermits—at least some of them—were "knowledgeable", "well instructed". He admired and supported libraries furnished with the best spiritual books. "There one can dedicate himself to leisure that is occupied and activity that is tranquil." These associations go beyond a play on words. They convey his ideal.

It is Bruno's taste for balance that gives the word *beneficial* its somewhat unusual meaning, but it is a meaning that recurs so frequently in his writing that it can be considered one of the key words of his thought. There is a very good example in his letter to Raoul le Verd: "It is not easy to give sound, beneficial advice all the time. Divine love, being more sound, is more beneficial. What is more sound and more beneficial, what more innate and more in accord with human nature, than to love the good?" With great insight the author of "Letters of the First Carthusians" observed: "A whole philosophy is there, or better, a whole theology. Bruno based a moral order, even the supernatural relationship of man with God, upon the very nature of things. 'Beneficial' is what allows nature to achieve the purpose that God has assigned to it, and this intrinsic purpose gives *nature its fulfillment*." To put this theological explanation in the terms of spiritual psychology, the meaning of *beneficial* is in harmony with balance, that balance that is a kind of alliance of the human with grace, creation, and redemption in a harmonious hierarchy of values. Thus, Bruno harmonizes solitude and friendship, learning and silence, strictness and affection, "athletic" competition and quiet.

He described the location and the climate of Calabria in lyrical, almost romantic terms: "How could I speak satisfactorily about this solitude, its agreeable location, its healthful and temperate climate?" etc. Of course, this "location", this "vast, pleasant plain", these "pasturelands adorned with flowers", etc., are agreeable to him only because they are, in the first place, a solitude.

Some are surprised perhaps that, in this letter to Raoul, Bruno does not once speak explicitly about self-discipline, fasting, and sacrifices. Only the phrase "austere rule" evokes the sacrificial side of the eremitical life. In his view all of that must be subject to the spiritual enthusiasm, profound joy, and fullness of charity in a soul that grace stimulates to contemplate and imitate Jesus Christ in his death and Resurrection. One must be pleased by his request at the conclusion of this severe letter: "Please send me *The Life of Saint Remi*, because it is impossible to find a copy where we are." This hermit still remembers Rheims; this pure contemplative is moved by the memory of a past that he loved long ago. Like anyone else, he remains interested in a book that impressed him. In it he had no doubt discovered a source of true charity.

Fascinating as Bruno's letter to Raoul le Verd may be for understanding the conditions in which he and his band of hermits lived, there are also interesting references to the material circumstances of the hermitage in Calabria and even to Bruno's holiness. "Now I let you know—in the hope it will not displease you—that I am in good health [Bruno was approaching the age of seventy] and things are going as well as I could wish." He gave us an enthusiastic description of the location of Saint Mary of La Torre. Unfortunately, there was no equally descriptive one of Chartreuse. A comparison of the two surely would have been interesting.

Should an answer be given to an objection that might be made about this letter? Since it brings to mind Saint Jerome's famous epistle to the monk Heliodorus or the theme of Saint John Chrysostom's *Expositio in Psalmo IX*, some might think that the thoughts Bruno expressed here are more or less conventional phrases about solitude, contemplation, etc. Nothing could be further from the truth. Concealed behind these words are the gift of a life, the fervor of an existence. Undoubtedly Bruno the letter writer was employing rhetorical devices then in fashion when he followed famous models like those. But the ancient art of writing is taking thoughts that are common to everyone and treating them in a personal way. And in his letter to Raoul le Verd Bruno surely succeeded in infusing everything he said with the fervor of his own love for God, his spiritual joy, and his friendship for Raoul. His words expressed his whole heart: he said exactly what he thought, felt, and lived. One example should be enough. More than forty times he took quotations from the Bible, explicit and implicit, to support his argument. Far from concealing or blurring his feelings, or making them everybody's or nobody's, they reveal the path he was taking, as well as the sacred texts that "sang" in his heart, and the mysteries toward which his own temperament and God's grace were directing him. No, the letter to Raoul le Verd[6] is not an academic lesson. It discloses Bruno's soul.

Perhaps, if there were nothing besides this letter, there might be doubt about knowing all of Bruno's thoughts about the vocation to the contemplative life. Might he have been inclined to work out his plan and select only some of his thoughts to present them in a manner calculated to persuade his friend Raoul le Verd rather than to disclose his own deepest thoughts? In a word, was this for the public or just for one person? He did not know that his letters, like those of other celebrated people, were going to be read by any except those to whom they were addressed.

Still another letter of Bruno's has survived.[7] This one is addressed to the brethren at Chartreuse. It is very important, and it agrees perfectly with the letter to Raoul le Verd. Fur-

[6] Raoul le Verd did not understand Bruno's appeal. He was still provost. Upon the death of Manassès in 1106, he became archbishop of Rheims. In this election Raoul had a formidable rival, the candidate put forward by the King of France. Both of these candidates had their supporters. Among those who opposed Raoul was a cleric who remembered Bruno's letter. In a pamphlet he accused him of being unfaithful to his vow to enter religion. He even used phrases from Bruno's letter. Raoul died in July 1124 and was buried in the abbey church of Saint-Remi. His name was inscribed in the necrology of the monks, a fact that seems to indicate that he had received the monastic habit *ad succurendum* during his last illness.

[7] While saying this we do not forget that we have two other sources of comparison to gain and appreciate Bruno's thoughts: the letter of Guigo about the solitary life (*Lettres des premiers Chartreux*, pp. 142–50) and Chapter LXXX of *Customs*. From these three texts, so different in tonality and literary genre, comes a wonderfully unified notion of the pure contemplative life.

thermore, the circumstances in which it was written, carried, and delivered make it even more impressive. The first Carthusians regarded this letter as Bruno's last testament to his sons at Chartreuse as well as the finest testimony of the attachment of Chartreuse to him, a testimony sealed by the death of Landuino.

The occasion of this letter? Landuino, whom Bruno had named prior over the hermits at Chartreuse before leaving for Rome in 1090, came to visit him at Saint Mary of La Torre in 1099 or 1100. It is a long way from the Dauphiné to Calabria; at that time the journey could be dangerous—and unfortunately it proved to be so—because some countries had been ravaged by war and overrun by the troops of Emperor Henry IV and the antipope Guibert of Ravenna. So, why did he undertake the journey? The letter does not say why. Chartreuse was a zealous community, and it seems the influence Bruno said wandering monks were having on some lay brothers was limited, though not negligible.[8] It is possible that Landuino went down to Calabria simply because he wanted to see Bruno again, whom all at Chartreuse considered to be their "only father" and their "superior",[9] and to discuss with him the present conditions at Chartreuse and its future more deeply than he could by letter or messenger.

Bruno was growing old, and Landuino himself was feeling the effect of various infirmities. Both of them—and all the brethren at Chartreuse—would welcome one last meeting. But Landuino died, and Bruno lived for a long time.

Noticing the poor state of Landuino's health, Bruno first thought of keeping him there with him, at least for a while;

[8] Cf. below, p. 155.

[9] *Eulogy* of the Grande Chartreuse.

but Landuino insisted on returning to Chartreuse, where his brethren were waiting for him and hoping for firsthand news from Bruno. He would not have had too much trouble persuading Bruno, who had not forgotten the events of his own departure in 1090.

Landuino was carrying a letter from Bruno for the community. But on his way through the north of Italy, he fell into the hands of supporters of the antipope who tried to force him to acknowledge Guibert as the lawful head of the Church; but no threat, promise, trick or act of violence could make him agree to that. Landuino affirmed his loyalty to Urban II, and they kept him prisoner for several months. On September 8, 1100, when Guibert died, Landuino was released; but, now very weak and unable to continue his journey, he took shelter in the nearby monastery of Saint Andrew "at the foot of Mount Sirapte", where, on September 14, 1100, seven days after he was given his freedom, he died.[10] The letter that Bruno had written to his sons at Chartreuse reached them, however, delivered either by Landuino's traveling companions who escaped from the supporters of Guibert or by someone Landuino entrusted with it before he died. One can imagine the reverence with which the hermits of Chartreuse received that letter, which was precious to them for two reasons.

This is the text of it:

> 1. Brother Bruno, to his brethren in Christ, beloved more than anything in the world: greeting in the Lord.
>
> Through our dear brother Landuino's account, so detailed and so consoling, I have learned of your uncompromising yet wise observance, so commendable and deserving of praise.

[10] We have these details from the very ancient Chronicle of the priors of Chartreuse.

He spoke to me about your holy love, your untiring zeal for purity of heart and virtue. My spirit rejoices in the Lord. Yes, I rejoice, I give praise and thanks to the Lord, at the same time that I sigh with sorrow. I rejoice, yes—it is right that I should—to see you grow in virtue; but I am distressed and blush, being so sluggish and neglectful in the misery of my sins.

2. Rejoice, my dear brothers, over your blessed vocation and the generous gift of divine grace you have received. Rejoice over having escaped the turbulent waters of this world, where there are so many perils and shipwrecks. Rejoice over having reached the peaceful quiet of a sheltered cove. Many desire to arrive there; many even tried to attain it, but did not arrive. Many did not remain after experiencing it, because they had not received that grace from God.

Also, my brothers, take it as certain and proven: no one, after having enjoyed so desirable a good, can ever give it up without regrets, if he is serious about the salvation of his soul.

3. This I say about you, my beloved brothers: my soul glorifies the Lord, when I consider the wonders of his mercy toward you after hearing the report of your dear father, your Prior, who is filled with joy and pride because of you. I, too, rejoice because, even though you do not read, almighty God with his own finger has written love and the knowledge of his holy law in your hearts. By your works you show what you love and what you know. With all possible care and zeal you practice true obedience, which is doing the will of God, the key and the seal of all spiritual observance, and that could never be without great humility and outstanding patience accompanied by a chaste love for the Lord and true charity. It is clear that you are wisely reaping the sweet and refreshing fruits of the Divine Scriptures.

4. Therefore, my brothers, remain in the condition you are in, and flee as from a pestilence those deceitful laymen who

seek to corrupt you, distributing their writings and whispering into your ear things that they neither understand nor love and which they contradict by their words and their acts. They are idle gyrovagues[11] who disgrace every good religious and think they should be praised for defaming those who really deserve praise, while they despise rules and obedience.

5. I would like to keep brother Landuino with me because he is often seriously ill. But because he feels he cannot find health, or joy, or life, or any improvement without you, he disagrees with me. His tears and sighs for your sake have shown me what you are to him and how much he loves all of you in perfect charity. I do not want to force him to stay, because I do not want to hurt him, or you, who are so dear to me on account of the merit of your virtues. That, my brothers, is why I urge you, I humbly but energetically beg you to show by your deeds the charity that you nourish in your hearts for him who is your beloved Father and Prior and tactfully and attentively providing for him whatever his numerous infirmities require. Perhaps he will decline to accept your loving services, preferring to endanger his health and his life rather than mitigate in any way the strictness of exterior observance, which of course could not be permitted; but that will no doubt be because he who is first in the community would blush to find himself last in observance and because

[11] Gyrovagues are the wandering monks who were living in the first spurs of the mountain of Chartreuse, who go about begging. Their unsettled life was sometimes an annoyance for the first hermits of Chartreuse, until Saint Hugh, the bishop of Grenoble, expelled them (*Lettres*, p. 87, n. 1). Guigo recalled those vexations with some bitterness at the time of the donation of Currière to the Carthusians: "These contentious and unstable men disguised as religious . . . it would take too long to tell how much they have troubled and distressed us, or how much kindness and help they have received from us" (*Annals of the Carthusian Order*, I, 322). It would be interesting to know what those "writings" were that the Gyrovagues "distributed". Cf. *Customs*, chap. 36.

he would fear to be the one among you to become lax and lukewarm on account of weakness. In my opinion, there is no reason to fear that. So that you will not be deprived of this grace, I authorize you to take my place in this one matter: you have permission to oblige him, respectfully, to take everything you give him for his health.

6. As regards myself, know that what I desire most after God is to go to see you. And as soon as I can, I will, with the help of God.

Farewell.[12]

Those who enjoy paradoxes will note that the most interesting thing about this letter is what it does not say: that it was in fact written in 1099 or 1100 and that it was carried by Landuino, the prior of Chartreuse; that ten years after Bruno left Chartreuse, Landuino felt a need to talk to Bruno and undertook that long and perilous journey; that, when Landuino was leaving, Bruno felt a desire to write in his own hand to his sons at Chartreuse, adding to the news that Landuino would give them orally; that Landuino, while he was in captivity or dying, saved that letter and had it delivered to the community at Chartreuse. Those facts reveal more about the relations of Bruno with Landuino and the Chartreuse than any treatise could. In addition, there are the tone of the letter, the fervor of the friendship, the masculine tenderness of Bruno's words, as well as the authority of his advice and the orders he gave concerning Landuino's health.

Clearly Bruno, through the venerable person of Landuino, remained the "father", the founder, the master, the model. It is not likely that such a strong a bond between Bruno and his sons at Chartreuse could be sustained during their separation had they not been communicating either by

[12] *Lettres des premiers Chartreux*, vol. I, pp. 82–90.

letters or messengers or mutual friends who were traveling. Here is one example from December 1095, while the Pope was in France. After Bruno's departure, Hugh of Grenoble was even more attentive—if that were possible—to the development of the Chartreuse. He went down to Italy as far as Apulia, into the territory of Duke Roger, where illness kept him for two years. During all that time would he not have met Bruno, with whom he enjoyed such a great friendship? The letter to Raoul le Verd also reveals that Bruno often entrusted letters to messengers on their way to France. Would not some of those letters have been for the sons whom he calls here *unice dilectis in Cristo* (brothers beloved in Christ)? Finally, it is known that in the middle of the thirteenth century Chartreuse still possessed a volume that contained the *Customs* of Guigo, the Chronicle *Magister*, and a number of letters that "clearly show that [Landuino] acknowledged Bruno to be the head [*prelatum*] and super-prior [*priorem majorem*] of Chartreuse". Those letters, preserved with so much respect and veneration that someone was bold enough to add them to Guigo's *Customs*, must have been letters that Bruno had written from Calabria. That volume, unfortunately, has never been found. It must have disappeared during one of the first fires that ravaged the hermitage of Chartreuse and caused irreparable damage to the hermits' library.

This letter to the brethren at Chartreuse, more brief, more familiar, more spontaneous than the letter to Raoul le Verd, contains some minor items that should receive more attention. It is essentially a joyful letter praising and giving thanks to the Lord. Bruno is rejoicing, and he invites his brethren at Chartreuse to rejoice: "*Gaudete*".[13] To express his joy he

[13] This repeated *Gaudete* recalls the *Gaudete . . . iterum dico: gaudete* of Saint Paul to his beloved Philippians (4:4).

uses the Virgin's words in the Magnificat. To everyone he says: "My spirit rejoices in the Lord", and especially to the lay brothers, "My soul glorifies the Lord!"

Why was Bruno's heart so full of joy? Because, through the account Landuino gave him, he understood that God was spreading over Chartreuse "the lavish gift of divine grace", "the wonders of his mercy". The generosity that God was showing to his sons stirred their father's heart to still more joy considering that he "regret[s] and blush[es] to remain sluggish and neglectful in the misery of [his] sins".

How did Bruno know that God was working marvels in the souls of his sons? They were generously and zealously pursuing their vocation as hermits, as they had all together once determined to do. In a few words Bruno gives us the essence of his ideal. At the heart of this vocation, there is always that pure, total, "chaste love for the Lord", as he wrote in the letter to Raoul, that "true charity" (*vera caritas*). That, according to Bruno, is the essential quality of the contemplative life.

How is this love manifested? There are elements here that did not appear in the letter to Raoul le Verd because that was not the place for them. Especially there is the striking expression that contains all of Bruno's spiritual balance: "I have learned of your uncompromising yet wise (*rationabilis*) observance that is so commendable and praiseworthy." The whole spirit of Bruno's rule is there, as well: the rules for observance must be "human", "reasonable", "possible". Perfection is not found in an abundance of observances, which many would find impossible, but in each and every one's taking the pains to practice carefully observances that are moderate. This it is that gives each community its vitality.

The soul of observance is obedience. Bruno congratulates his lay brothers, writing: "With all possible care and zeal you practice true obedience, which is doing the will of God, the key and the seal of all spiritual observance." That is certainly one of Master Bruno's most beautiful directives. He gives it at the end of his long experience of the contemplative life. Because of this single phrase endless thanks are due him from his first sons and from everyone.

Landuino gave him the opportunity to provide a marvelous example of what he understood observance and obedience to be. Brother Landuino "often is seriously ill". Bruno does not doubt that the charity the brethren at Chartreuse have for their "beloved father and Prior" will "tactfully and attentively provide whatever his numerous infirmities require". But he fears that Landuino will decline, preferring "to endanger his health and his life rather than mitigate in any way the strictness of exterior observance". That, in itself, would be unacceptable, but Bruno understands Landuino's conscience: "He who is first in the community would blush to find himself last in observance", and "he would fear to be the one among you to become more lax and lukewarm on account of weakness". What an insight into the spirit then prevailing among the hermits that Bruno could write such things to the community at Chartreuse! Obedience will regulate the difference between observance and charity. Bruno delegates his own authority to the community of Chartreuse in, he specifies, "this one matter" about Landuino. "You have permission to oblige him, respectfully, to take everything you give him for his health."

Could there be any testimony more personal or touching about the spirit that Bruno knew how to inspire in a group of hermits, as well as his goodness and his firm gentleness?

Another important insight about obedience is given in this letter to the brethren at Chartreuse. The letter, which is addressed to the whole community, contains one passage that pertains especially to the lay brothers. Bruno speaks of obedience, and in the context his concept of obedience stands out with special power and precision. The contemplative life, as Bruno envisages it, is nourished by the Holy Scriptures. But the lay brother does not study. He comes unrefined, unlettered, unable to read the sacred texts. The marvel of obedience is that it supplies for learning. It is learning, and, at the same time, it is love. It allows the least educated of the lay brothers to "reap the sweet and refreshing fruits of the Divine Scriptures", and it leads them directly to the contemplation that "cultured men" strive for by their study of holy books. "I, too, rejoice because, even though you do not read, almighty God with his own finger has written love and the knowledge of his holy law in your hearts. By your works you show what you love and what you know." This formula, so concise, so beautiful, deserves a long commentary.

As in his letter to Raoul le Verd, Bruno here emphasized the climate in which a contemplative life develops and is pursued with fervor. One phrase sums up his thought: "The security of a sheltered cove". "Rejoice over having escaped the turbulent waters of this world, where there are so many perils and shipwrecks. Rejoice that you have reached the peaceful quiet and security of a sheltered cove." A problem of perseverance and courage, no doubt: "Many desire to arrive there, many even try to attain it, but did not arrive." But it is a matter of grace and vocation: "Many, too, did not remain after experiencing it, because they had not received that grace from God." And here Bruno makes a statement that at first appears very daring in the absolute form he gives it, which rests upon his more than fifteen years of experience in the wilderness: "No one, after having enjoyed so desirable a good, can ever *give it up without experiencing regrets*[14] if he is serious about the salvation of his soul."

There they are, similar in depth, different in expression and tonality, the two letters of Bruno that survive. One argues, tries to convince, and leads to a conclusion; the other expresses joy and paternal affection. Both reveal Bruno as wise and sensible, more concerned about works of generosity, about gentle and constant perseverance, than about ephemeral flights of fervor. In a marvelous harmony he brings together things that at first appear mutually exclusive or that at least would not be reconciled by themselves, such as effort and quiet, austerity and the joy of creation, uncompromising observance and fraternal mercy. All that, along with the enormous goodness that radiates from Bruno's entire personality, surrounds him with a quiet enthusiasm for this very special vocation, the vocation of the contemplative. This vocation is a call to love God with a love that is pure and "chaste" (*castus amor*), lived and savored in solitude, silence, and simplicity. It is an anticipation of seeing God face to face throughout eternity. It is a sample of the absolute peace that will be found in heaven. The spiritual sense that Bruno gives to the word is the complete opposite of self-centeredness:

"Rejoice that you have reached the . . . security of a sheltered cove."

[14] Author's italics.

IX

Calabria and Chartreuse

Surely Bruno himself was living and helping others at Saint Mary of La Torre to live the particular kind of ideal contemplative life, both practical and theoretical, that he described in the two letters he wrote from Calabria. Lack of reliable documents leaves what happened during those years at Calabria uncertain, with the result that ingenious biographers have invented opportunities to make him known and active in the Church. But, except for the location and political conditions, Bruno's ten years in Calabria seem to have been just like the six years in Chartreuse: the same exterior silence, the same relish for solitude, the same zeal for the contemplative life, the same spiritual inspiration for his community, the same simple goodness, the same charity.

During the difficult developments that befell the Calabria foundation after Bruno's death, one thing was certain: there would always be a group of hermits faithful to the ideal of Bruno. The number in this group would diminish, but it would continue and preserve his spirit. Thus, around the year 1170 some solitaries who were living in Piedmont near Garessio asked the "master of the wilderness" (the Prior of Saint Mary of La Torre) to have some of his religious come to form them in the eremitical life. The Prior complied with their wish and sent them several of his sons. But when they finished their novitiate they asked to join Chartreuse, not Saint Mary of La Torre. In their choice it is hard not to see the influence of the Calabrian hermits' faithfulness to Bruno's pure ideal. Also, when William of Messina, the last superior of Saint Mary of La Torre and of Saint Stephen, requested and obtained affiliation of his monastery with the Cistercian Order, the hermits who were still at Saint Mary objected and finally departed for Aspromonte, some thirty miles below Reggio—the supreme testimony of fidelity to Bruno made by some of his sons 100 years after the foundation.

Today it is even clearer how important it was that history definitely record that no cenobium, no cenobitic life at all had existed either at Saint Mary of La Torre or near it during Bruno's lifetime. What would be the meaning of the letter to Raoul le Verd and the letter to the community at Chartreuse if they had been written by a Bruno who was himself unfaithful to his original plan? The location and the political conditions in Calabria that have been mentioned were different from those at Chartreuse. These differences had great influence over the destiny of the hermitage in Calabria. They were already making notable changes in the life of the hermits during Bruno's lifetime. There should be at least a brief reference to that situation.

At the beginning of the Chartreuse foundation, Bruno had obtained clear title to the property, though all kinds of interference and rudeness on the part of the donors began then. There, on those poor lands, isolated, so unproductive that no nobleman and no abbey wanted them, he had complete freedom to do whatever he wanted. If Hugh of Grenoble stood by the hermits, if he came to intervene in their affairs, it was to help them keep their spirit. He thoroughly understood Bruno's ideal and made it his own. Independence was considered so essential that in 1090, as soon as the community had come together again, Bruno and Landuino didn't stop until they had regained complete control over the property where the hermitage was established.

In Calabria things were very different. In addition to the fact that the location of the hermitage, like the landscape itself, was less inaccessible, less secluded, and less wild than Chartreuse, Bruno and his sons were willingly or unwillingly committed to them by Count Roger and by him alone. Their installation at the beginning and the fine grants that the prince made for them later were, whether Bruno wished it or not, part of a policy to replace Greek monasticism with Latin monasticism in that area. In the complicated diplomacy of Urban II, Bruno was an intermediary, a mediator, if not actually a hostage held by the Pope and the Count. He would not be able to resist the Count without displeasing the Pope. But there was no suggestion of that. The high regard that the Count had for Bruno was known and respected by everyone. The two men were bound by particularly cordial ties. In his dealings with the Count Bruno unquestionably enjoyed a place of privilege. Biographers have used the word *friendship*, and produced an entire literature dedicated to this attachment between the prince and the saint. People like to quote a verse written by Maraldus, a religious of La Torre, for the occasion when Bruno baptized Roger II, the Count's son, who later wore the crown of the Two Sicilies. In fact, it is not certain that the relationship of Bruno and the prince ever went beyond an *courtoise entente* (a very friendly understanding).

Whatever it was, that perfect accord between Bruno and Count Roger gave rise to two series of events that appeared unrelated to Bruno's ideal for hermits but that, in the long run, were a threat to his work. The Count continued his donations to the hermitage, and the *Magister eremi* (master of the desert) little by little became one of the principal figures in the Count's "realm".

Following are the principal stages in the settlement of the hermitage property during Bruno's lifetime. That many of the official acts were made in the two names of Bruno and Lanuino leads to some clear conclusions.

The first document donating the wilderness of La Torre has not been found, but there is no doubt that it existed. Indicating the importance of the donation are the documents of confirmation issued by the Bishop of Squillace on December 7, 1091; of Pope Urban II on October 14, 1092; and of Count Roger on May 10, 1093. All the land surrounding La Torre "for two miles around the church" was given to the hermits. The land, right from the beginning, was therefore extensive.[1]

On August 15 (1094?) Argiro, archbishop of Palermo, solemnly consecrated the church of the hermitage under the title of the Virgin Mary and Saint John the Baptist. The Count and his court honored the ceremony by their presence. In the entourage of Argiro were four bishops: Tristan, bishop of Tropea; Augero, bishop of Catania; Theodore, bishop of Squillace; and Godfrey, bishop of Milazzo. To celebrate the event, Count Roger made a new and important donation to the hermitage: namely, the ancient monastery of Arsafia with all its dependencies, property that extended as far as the village of Squillace.

[1] A circle of "two miles around the church" was about 2,750 hectares (6,790 acres). The first donation of Chartreuse was about 1,700 (4,209 acres). But at Chartreuse practically none of the land could be used for anything, very different from the land at Calabria.

On September 4 (1094?) Count Roger gave Bruno and Lanuino thirteen families of farmworkers as vassals. The Count as well as the Duke made other gifts of "vassal families", fifty at one time and sixteen at another.

In 1096 the Count gave Lanuino a mill. In the same year he gave Bruno and Lanuino the orchard of Saint Nicholas and a large property whose owner "died without heir".

On June 16, 1101, shortly before his death, the Count gave Bruno and Lanuino the village of Aruncio, which was on the lands of Squillace, as well as a hundred "serfs" who belonged either to that village or to two others named Montauro and Oliviana, which he had already given to the hermits. To them he added the mill "Alexi", which was near Squillace.[2]

All this abundance was very different from the poverty at Chartreuse. In 1101, the property at Chartreuse had increased hardly at all. The land remained poor and hard to cultivate, and so, to survive there, the hermits had to be few—they were still no more than twelve. But in Calabria they were thirty already, and their lands were extensive and prosperous. How would the *Magister eremi* fail to become a

[2] Modern criticism of the documents of Calabria finds unexpected corroboration in a document of the twelfth century. Around 1144 Roger II, son of Count Roger and first King of Sicily and Calabria, began a project of verifying and confirming all the privileges of the churches and subjects in his kingdom as part of his general plan of administrative reorganization. The "master of the church of Saint Mary of the Hermits" had to give the King's officials their diplomas or titles of donation. By chance, the list of acts has been preserved, and a summary of each is in the great document by which, on November 5, 1144, Roger II confirmed all the privileges of Bruno's sons. The acts on this list are the very ones that appear authentic when examined in the light of current critical methods. Four other acts have been lost. The acts that today seem to deserve to be rejected as spurious are not found on the list drawn up for Roger II by his officials.

man of influence in the kingdom? If the archives have not preserved any pontifical document entrusting some apostolic mission to Bruno,[3] it was otherwise for Lanuino. In 1104 Pope Paschal II instructed him to see to the choice of a bishop for Miletus and to the correction of two prevaricating abbots. Several times between 1104 and 1118 Paschal entrusted Lanuino with the reformation of certain monasteries—particularly delicate assignments that reveal Lanuino's authority as well as his talents for managing matters. In February of 1113, he was given the noteworthy privilege of receiving candidates into the novitiate and to profession without requesting permission from their bishop. While the influence of Bruno's successors was increasing gradually, there was a certain disquiet growing up among the hermits. As they departed from Bruno's simplicity and silence, they also lost his peace—that peace that is essential for pure contemplation.

There is another fact to remember from these original charters: namely, that in most of them the name of Lanuino is added to the name of Bruno. A Carthusian enumerated them. "Of fifteen charters from the counts, two bulls and one letter from Urban II, and a privilege of Paschal II, fourteen are addressed jointly to Bruno and Lanuino, as if the two of them were equal superiors of the foundation in Calabria. Three documents are addressed only to Bruno; two, only to Lanuino. Of these nineteen, four attributed an active role in administration to Lanuino." That means Lanuino was not merely one who substituted for Prior Bruno; rather, in negotiations and in relations with those outside the monastery, Lanuino was Bruno's alter ego. Of course, Bruno's entire

[3] The nomination of Jean of Nicéphore as bishop of Squillace can hardly be counted. It was said that the choice was made "on the advice of two holy people: Bruno and our brother Lanuino".

life manifested his dislike of administration. In Chartreuse, the charity and the discretion of Bishop Hugh of Grenoble made up for that deficiency. Again, Bruno's haste in giving the property of Chartreuse to the abbey of Chaise-Dieu entirely and immediately when Urban II's appeal stirred up a crisis among his companions at the hermitage also showed him incapable of the prudence and subtleties needed in affairs of the world. For the many complicated donations at Calabria, he had to have someone skilled in such matters, a companion upon whom he could rely to assume all the worries of administration: and right there was Lanuino, that Norman who would one day succeed him as "master of the wilderness" and who seems to have had a character active, dynamic, and realistic, as well as genuine gifts for contemplation—the Church later beatified him.

That division of responsibilities, though surely required by circumstances, brought some serious inconveniences. Presumed to be a faithful and exemplary disciple, a man like Lanuino, who was given the administration of considerable property, could not have the same view of things as Bruno, who was contemplative, poor, and detached. Furthermore Bruno, with his facility in spiritual matters, would have had to perceive that such wealth and such cares were not in harmony with his ideal for the hermitage. As long as he was present with his goodness, his balance, and his clear vision of contemplative life, these discrepancies were only shadows, quickly eliminated in the radiance of his personality. But what of the day when he would no longer be there?

The documents reveal some of the differences between Bruno's approach and Lanuino's in regard to accepting or requesting a gift.

There is not a single document indicating that Bruno requested a gift. On the contrary, the famous document of the siege of Capua, which, though it is not genuine (it was written between 1122 and 1146) conveys some of the popular admiration for Bruno, showing that he refused the extravagant donations Count Roger wanted to make. The document reads as follows: "I, Roger, asked him to accept substantial revenues from my land at Squillace, but he declined. He said he had left his father's house and mine, where he had held the first place, to be able to serve God with a soul completely unencumbered by the goods of earth, which were foreign to him. Only with difficulty could I get him to accept a small gift from me. Nevertheless, I presented to him for himself and his successors in perpetuity the revenues from the monastery of Saint James at Montauro without any rent, as well as many other gifts and privileges. Letters have already been sent to execute all this." Since the charter is not genuine, this detail is no more impressive than the rest of the story; still, forgers generally perpetrate their frauds in circumstances that give them a semblance of truth. Would Bruno's refusal of the donations have been mentioned had his detachment not been part of his personality? In any case, it agrees too well with what is known of his concern for poverty, total detachment, and his care to spare his sons the "evil" of riches for it to be rejected entirely. And would he have written to Raoul le Verd about this matter, if he had been pleased to accept so much land and revenue in Calabria? That would have been hypocritical.

The other panel of the diptych shows Lanuino's reaction to the donations. Not only did he accept what was offered, but he asked for donations. No doubt their needs justified that, and sometimes even compelled them to beg. Still, he seems to have had a natural ability, which did not escape Count Roger's notice. There is a genuine document from 1096, in which the Norman finesse of "Brother Lanuino of the Wilderness" meets the no less Norman ingenuity of Count Roger. It was in the matter of a mill and a waterfall. No résumé could have the flavor of this direct quotation from Count Roger:

> One day I, Roger, by the grace of God Count of Calabria and Sicily, was out riding with some companions. It was after nine o'clock, and we were coming from Saint-Ange, when we met Brother Lanuino of the wilderness, who was going up to the main square beside the road to Gramatico. Lanuino rode with us past Saint-Ange and then asked me to stop for a while, saying he wanted to speak with me about something that would interest me. We stopped at the chapel called Saint-Larron, on the little hill which is beyond Saint-Ange. Using the very words of Master Bruno—for he was a man I could let convince me easily—he asked me to give them one of the mills of Squillace for the shepherds of the monastery at Montauro (?). Out of regard for Master Bruno I answered him pleasantly: "Brother Lanuino, by God's grace you are a capable craftsman and a remarkable builder of monasteries. Get busy and build your mill over by Severatum on the estate of Arsafia, which has been given to you. There you will find a very fine waterfall." Lanuino then remembered an old mill that used to be there. Giving thanks to God, he asked me to give him the old mill and to have a document drawn up and sealed with my seal. I did this, asking all my companions to be witnesses. Later, my wife, the Countess Adelaide, concurred with this during a great celebration at the palace of Melitus, during which Brother Lanuino and my son Malgerius accepted this charter. The guests, cupbearers, and equestrians all shouted: Amen, let it be done.[4]

This document would deserve to be studied in detail. It reflects characteristics of the time; better than any expla-

[4] *Placitum Comitis Rogerii*, Tromby, *Storia*, T. II, App. II, p. 75, no. XI.

nation could, it describes the relationship of Count Roger to Bruno and Lanuino. Over this legal document hovers an amused, ironic smile. Count Roger was not deceived by the monk Lanuino's tactic, but out of regard for Bruno he agreed. At any rate, Lanuino was completely revealed, both by the Count's words *bonus laborator* (a capable builder of monasteries) and by his own reaction. He is not like Bruno. This document, which is definitely genuine, allows a more accurate interpretation of what truth there is in the inauthentic one mentioned above. In the charter about the siege of Capua, Bruno appeared to be detached, poor, and reluctant to receive extravagant donations, while Lanuino gladly accepted what the Count offered, twice even insisting that the gifts be increased. As business sense and negotiating skill characterize the "Lanuino of legend", so concern about poverty distinguishes the "Bruno of legend".[5]

In passing, and with all the reservations that this charter's lack of authenticity imposes, it is very surprising that the differing attitudes of Bruno and Lanuino are given by reference to a donation in the territory of Squillace. This territory, which Bruno had refused to accept on August 2, 1099, had been given to the hermits already, some of it on August 15 (1094?) and some on June 16, 1101. It was precisely at Montauro, in the region of Squillace, that on January 27, 1114, with the authorization of the Pope, that Lanuino erected a *cenobium* (a monastery of cenobites) with the rule of Benedict. That was the beginning of the evolution that took the hermitage at Saint Mary of La Torre away from Bruno's ideal and made it a Cistercian monastery.

[5] Bruno and Lanuino in the presence of Count Roger are reminiscent of Elisha and Gehazi in the presence of Naaman: Elisha completely disinterested and behind his back his servant Gehazi begging gifts from Naaman! (cf. 2 Kings 5).

This divergence between the vision and attitude of Bruno and that of Lanuino could not escape the notice of the community in Calabria. Disagreement among the religious was inevitable, and it broke out over the election of his successor soon after Bruno died. Many were reluctant to have Lanuino named as prior at Calabria. The matter was serious enough and lasted long enough to need the intervention of the Pope. Paschal II appointed the Cardinal of Albano as his legate to study the situation and reestablish peace. In the end, Lanuino was elected "master of the wilderness", and all of the religious promised obedience to him. Nevertheless, through letters that he wrote to the hermits to recognize the return of peace, the Pope judged it proper to entreat Lanuino to imitate Bruno's virtues, particularly his faithfulness to the hermitage. But that is another story.

X

The Death of Bruno

Death was about to affect Bruno's friendships and relationships. In less than two years he would experience the loss of three people with whom he had close ties. On July 29, 1099, Urban II died. Fourteen days after that Jerusalem was liberated, but Godfrey of Bouillon's messengers arrived from Rome too late to tell the Pope. Succeeding him on August 14, 1099, was Rainier, an elderly monk of Cluny and cardinal priest of the church of Saint Clement, who took the name of Paschal II. He was Bruno's friend, and he had great esteem for his foundation. In July of 1101 Paschal II confirmed the donations that Count Roger had made to the hermits of Calabria.

In September of 1100 Bruno received, like repeated blows, the news that Landuino was captured, then that he was set free, and finally that he died. Landuino's faithfulness to the lawful Pope must have filled him with joy and pride. But his death brought sorrow—Landuino, the companion during all those first hours, the faithful friend to whom he confided his trials and joys, the disciple to whom he could confidently entrust his foundation at Chartreuse at the emotional moment when he departed for Rome. If Landuino died far from his Father and far from his sons, was it not because of his faithfulness as a son in undertaking that long and dangerous journey for the sake of seeing him?

The time came on June 21, 1101, for Count Roger also to die, that successful fighter and notable administrator. The whole foundation of the house in Calabria was bound up with his name. He was Bruno's patron, a trifle too determined and almost too generous. His generosity, though, was sincere, coming from a genuine desire to ensure the presence of the hermits in Calabria for a long time to come.

But what could finally come of the hope Bruno expressed at the end of his letter to the brothers at Chartreuse: "As regards myself, know that what I desire most after God is to go to see you. And as soon as I can, I will do it, with the help of God". He surely had no illusion about that any longer. Now only the greatest desire remained, which, according to his own words, he had cherished for sixteen years: the desire to keep "a vigilant watch" in the solitude, his desire for God.

Nothing is known about the illness that brought on his death. There is only that round-robin letter that his sons at Calabria wrote at the beginning of the Necrology saying his death was very peaceful. During the preceding week, Bruno was eager to make his profession of faith, a common practice there at the time. The letter reads as follows:

> Knowing that the hour had come for him to pass from this world to the Father, [Bruno] called his brothers together, reviewed all the stages of his life since infancy, and recalled the special events of his lifetime. Then, in a profound, detailed discourse he expressed his faith in the Trinity, concluding with these words: "I believe also in the sacraments that the Church believes and holds in reverence, and particularly that the bread and wine which are consecrated on the altar are, after the Consecration, the true Body of our Lord Jesus Christ,

> his true Flesh and his real Blood, which we receive for the forgiveness of our sins and in the hope of eternal life." The following Sunday, the evening before the ninth of October in the year of our Lord 1101, his holy soul left his body.

No commentary can improve on that kind of simplicity.

For a long time the complete text of Bruno's profession of faith was lost. Dom Constantius of Rigetis found it in the archives of Saint Mary of La Torre. Unfortunately the manuscript was in very bad condition, nibbled on, with parts difficult to make out. Dom Constantius transcribed the text and sent it to the general of the Carthusians in 1522. Here is his translation, which appeared in the critical edition of *Sources chrétiennes*. It begins with a moving prologue by the brothers of Calabria: "We have carefully preserved Master Bruno's profession of faith, which he pronounced in the presence of all his assembled brothers, when he felt the time was approaching for him to go the way of all flesh, because he had urgently requested us to be witnesses of his faith before God." Here is his profession of faith:

> 1. I firmly believe in the Father, the Son, and the Holy Spirit: the Father unbegotten, the only begotten Son, the Holy Spirit proceeding from them both; and I believe that these three Persons are but one God.
>
> 2. I believe that the same Son of God was conceived by the Holy Spirit in the womb of the Virgin Mary. I believe that the Virgin was chaste before she bore her child, that she remained a virgin while she bore her child, and continued a virgin ever after. I believe that the same Son of God was conceived among men, a true man with no sin. I believe the same Son of God was captured by the hatred of some of the Jews who did not believe, was bound unjustly, covered with spittle, and scourged. I believe that he died, was buried, and descended into hell to free those of his who were held there.

He descended for our redemption, he rose again, he ascended into heaven, and from there he will come to judge the living and the dead.

3. I believe also in the sacraments that the Church believes and holds in reverence, and especially that what has been consecrated on the altar is the true Flesh and the true Blood of our Lord Jesus Christ, which we receive for the forgiveness of our sins and in the hope of eternal salvation. I believe in the resurrection of the flesh and everlasting life.

4. I acknowledge and believe the holy and ineffable Trinity, Father, Son, and Holy Spirit, to be but only one God, of only one substance, of only one nature, of only one majesty and power. We profess[1] that the Father was neither begotten nor created but that he has begotten. The Father takes his origin from no one; of him the Son is born and the Holy Spirit proceeds. He is the source and origin of all Divinity. And the Father, ineffable by his very nature, from his own substance has begotten the Son ineffably; but he has begotten nothing except what he is himself: God has begotten God, light has begotten light, and it is from him that all Fatherhood in heaven and on earth proceeds. Amen.[2]

Two comments should be made about this document. The first concerns the design of the profession of faith. A comparison of this text with the quotations from the letter of the brothers of Calabria, which was cited above, shows the former concludes with a statement about the sacraments, and this one with a statement about the Fatherhood of God and the Trinity. This difference would be of little importance if this last statement did not elsewhere reproduce, word for

[1] From this point on the saint "recites" the profession of faith of the Council of Toledo, which explains the shift to the first person plural. The Creed of the Council is written in the first person plural (N.D.T.).

[2] *Lettres des Premiers Chartreux*, I, pp. 90–93.

word, a passage of the Creed of the Eleventh Council of Toledo (November 7, 675). So, one wonders: Was this passage inserted into Bruno's profession of faith at a later date? Recent studies by historians of the Carthusian Order lead to a different conclusion. The foundation in Calabria was in an area where part of the population was of Greek origin. Through his goodness and sense of balance, Bruno succeeded in bringing Latin monks and Greek monks together to live in the same community—an achievement that was not easy to accomplish at that time. The presence of these two groups would explain the two trinitarian Creeds in his profession of faith. In the first, Bruno expressed his faith in the Trinity by avowing that the Holy Spirit proceeds from the Father and from the Son; in the second, he added the beautiful Creed of the Council of Toledo, which, by emphasizing the Fatherhood of God, gave the Catholic Faith an expression more acceptable to the Greek spirit.

Now the second comment. Bruno's profession of faith is one of a great contemplative. It complements what the two letters (the one to Raoul le Verd and the one to the brothers of Chartreuse) revealed earlier about his original vocation. These seem to be the deepest fruits of his contemplation in the wilderness. In admiration and love his soul is established upon the pillars of the four great, profound mysteries of the Christian life: the mystery of the Fatherhood of God, the mystery of the Eucharist, the mystery of the Incarnation and the Passion, and the mystery of Mary, the ever Virgin Mother. To abide among them was his pleasure, his life, his joy. At the hour of his death, he spontaneously fixed his last gaze on these revealed treasures. His lips spoke of what he had lived. More than a profession of faith, his words are a profession of love. He wished to die in the Light that had enlightened his entire life.

Bruno died on October 6, 1101, a little more than seventy years old, seventeen years after he founded the hermitage at Chartreuse. Hardly had his death been announced when people from Calabria and Italy streamed to pay respects to his earthly remains. It is said that the Carthusians allowed his body to lie in state for three days before burying it.

When an important person died, it was customary to send a messenger to churches and monasteries where he was known to announce his death and request prayers and suffrages for the repose of his soul. This messenger generally carried long scrolls of parchment (*Rotuli*, hence the name Rolliger, Rotuliger)[3] so that on it those who knew the deceased either directly or by reputation could write a eulogy and their promise to pray for him. After Bruno's death, the hermits of Calabria sent a scroll—delivered, no doubt, by a lay brother—to all the churches, abbeys, and convents where he was known. That messenger was the bearer of the round-robin letter that "announced Bruno's death and asked suffrages for his soul".

One hundred and seventy-eight of these *Eulogies* still exist. These documents make it possible to reconstruct the itinerary of the scroll, or at least determine where it stopped.

[3] Concerning the Scrolls of the Dead, see L. Delisle in the *Bibliothèque de l'École des Chartes*, T. III, 2nd series, pp. 371ff. There are still several difficult problems about Bruno's funeral scroll. It was found at the Chartreuse of Calabria at the time of the recovery of the monastery in 1514, and as early as the following year (1515) Dom Francis of Puy gave an edition of it to Amerbach at Basel. But the manuscript is clearly incomplete. Are the entries in the original order? Had anything been inserted from other funeral scrolls, particularly from the one of Blessed Vital, who died twenty-one years after Bruno? How were the seven famous verses by the hermits of Calabria introduced, beginning "Laudandus Bruno"? This is not the place to resolve these problems. In any case, Bruno's funeral scroll is certainly genuine, and that is enough for this volume.

From Calabria it went toward the north of Italy. It went to Lucca in Tuscany, then to Plaisance. Then it turned west and reached the Alps at Suse. By which pass did it cross the Alps? It appeared again at Oulx in the Dauphiné. It arrived at Grenoble, and from Grenoble it went to Chartreuse. On the Scroll of the Dead the hermits of Chartreuse wrote these sad, heartfelt lines:

> More than any others we, the brothers of Chartreuse, are afflicted and deprived of our consolation by the death of our beloved father, the renowned Bruno. How is it possible to put limits on what we will do for this holy soul, so dear to us? The good that we owe him will always outweigh anything we could do for him. Now and always we will pray for him as our only father and our master. As is proper for sons, we will not stop the Masses and the spiritual practices that we customarily offer for the dead.

Then the scroll came to the dependent priory of Chaise-Dieu called Cornillon, the major priory of the canons of Saint Ruf near Saint André, whose eulogy is particularly touching. Then to Lyons, Cluny, Cîteaux; to Molesmes, where the eulogy was written by the hand of Saint Robert; to Paris, to Chartres, and to Rheims, where five different eulogies were written for him; to Troyes, Laon, Rouen, Soissons, Arras, Orléans, Auxerre, Bayeux, Caen, etc. From France the scroll went to Belgium and through part of England. Did it travel by land or by sea? Why didn't it reach Cologne and its neighboring areas? The journey ended at Saint Mary's of Tropéa in Calabria. Two verses of the eulogy that was then written for Bruno indicate that the way the funeral scroll was unrolled and its present weight have frayed its neck and it cannot be transported any more:

Inde cutis colli teritur præ pondere rolli.
Rolligeri collum nequit ultra tollere rollum.[4]

The result of these texts, which of course are partly literary, is an incontestable testimony. Bruno was presented as exceptional, the "light of the clergy", "interpreter of the Scriptures", "guide of saints", the "teacher of teachers". In the *Eulogies* there are still more entries. If the author of the eulogy (whether a group or an individual) knew Bruno, lived with him, or at least had some contact with him, then admiration, great as it might be, would give way to affection, to gratitude, to a kind of tenderness. The verses that the hermits of Calabria dedicated to him are a good summary of the different characteristics that form the impression of exceptional goodness that radiated from him. "Bruno deserves to be praised for many things, but especially for this: his life was always the same. That was typical of him. He always had a smile on his face, always had a prudent word. To the severity of a father he joined the tenderness of a mother. Great he was, but everyone found him gentle as a lamb. In truth, he was the Israelite praised in the Gospel". Later when he was editing the Constitutions, Lambert, the third "master of the wilderness" of Calabria, again recalled Bruno's goodness.

Is it not significant that the same trait that Bruno is said to have loved to contemplate and praise in God—*O Bonitas!* the goodness of God![5]—was the one for which his contemporaries remembered him? What a mystery is the hidden yet radiant course of a soul! By what secret, personal attractions

[4] PL 152, 605.

[5] The basis for the tradition that ascribes the exclamation to Saint Bruno is not known. Nevertheless, it corresponds very well to what is known of his spiritual preferences from the texts cited above.

the Lord guides each one of us toward his destiny! "Master Bruno, a man of understanding heart". Describing him in this way, doesn't Guigo express Bruno's entire vocation in a single word: a natural gift, to which was added his vocation and grace, the very essence of his existence? He loved, and, when love attained a certain depth, where could he better find satisfaction than in solitude, silence, and the total gift of himself in sacrifice—the total simplicity of being that remains the surest approach to the living God?

After his death Bruno, like the other hermits, was buried in the cemetery of Saint Mary's. In 1101 or 1122, his body was transferred from the cemetery to the church of the hermitage, to a vault that still existed, though empty, when the Carthusians returned in 1514. Toward 1194, when the hermitage was abandoned in favor of the *cenobium* at Saint Stephen, Bruno's body was transferred from the church of Saint Mary and placed under the sanctuary of the church of Saint Stephen. When around 1502 or 1508 the Cistercians were thinking of returning their monastery to the Carthusians, Abbot Dom Pandolfo of Sabinis took up Bruno's relics and placed them in a nearby altar, which was behind and to the right of the high altar of Saint Stephen. When they returned on February 27, 1514, the Carthusians carried the relics to the sacristy, where they were officially authenticated on November 1, 1514. On the same day they were placed in a new reliquary and transferred to the same altar where they were before February 1514.

Meanwhile, by means of what the curia calls a verbal declaration, Pope Leo X had authorized the veneration of Saint Bruno. The Cardinal of Pavia, protector of the Carthusian Order who presided at the ceremony, describes the scene in a letter: "The holy Pope Leo X, saying that he had for a long time been hearing much about the glory and the holiness of the blessed confessor Bruno, judged it just and reasonable that he who had been adorned with such great gifts and such magnificent graces and who had received from the Almighty so docile a heart to carry out his precepts and keep the law of life and holiness, was venerated and honored in a manner worthy of him, now that he rejoices in divine glory for ever." This was authorized only for the Carthusians. It was by a bull of February 17, 1623, that Gregory XV extended the veneration of Saint Bruno to the entire Church. Bruno's destiny was finally established.

Epilogue: Bruno after Bruno

During the 1120s, Guigo I, the fifth prior of the Chartreuse, faced a delicate problem. Bruno had left his sons a living legacy but without a constitution. Bishop Hugh of Grenoble, who had helped Bruno and his first companions found the hermitage, now almost seventy years old, wanted to give a sound structure to Bruno's work and make it useful for the Church. He urged Guigo to write down a kind of rule for Carthusian life.

In 1115, on the advice of some of the religious of Chartreuse, two monks of the Benedictine abbey of Ambronay had started a new hermitage at Portes, near Belley. Not far from there, at Saint Sulpice-en-Bugey, another group of hermits was also trying to live according to the ideal of Bruno. Around 1116 four new groups had been formed: at Ecouges, in the diocese of Grenoble; at Durbon, in the diocese of Gap; at Sylve-Bénite, in the diocese of Vienne in the Dauphiné; and at Meyriat, where Ponce de Balmey, a canon of Lyons, had founded a hermitage for which Guigo had proposed Stephen of Bourg, one of Bruno's first companions, as prior. Stephen died in 1118, and Ponce, who had been trained at Chartreuse, was chosen to replace him. The hermitages took the risk of starting others, and several of them wanted a written rule for the eremitical life according to the ideal of Bruno. Those who asked Guigo to give them a rule were Bernard, prior of Portes; Humbert, prior of Saint-Sulpice; and Milon, who was prior of Meyriat after Ponce was elevated to be bishop of Belley. All of these requests were added to Hugh of Grenoble's advice.

This pressure created a real problem of conscience for Guigo. Didn't Bruno avoid founding a religious Order? Didn't he allow the house in Calabria to live on its own without ever connecting it to the Chartreuse? Didn't he intend for each hermitage to be under the jurisdiction of the local bishop? Besides, some of them had made no request. Were they—all of them Bruno's sons—going to make a distinction between one hermitage and another? And how was Guigo to make laws when Bruno had never made any? It was true that his brothers at Chartreuse had chosen him to be their prior after only eleven years at the young age of twenty-six. But did his thirteen years at Chartreuse permit him to write a Rule that would be imposed on monks, some of whom had longer and more extensive experience of the eremitical life than he had? And finally, since his temperament was so different from Bruno's, would he be the right one to interpret his thought? In the Prologue to the *Customs* he wrote with sincerity: "We did not believe we were the one who could or should undertake a task like this."

However, if someone had to draw up a rule for the eremitical life according to Bruno's ideal, the time was right. Bishop Hugh was still there to verify Bruno's intentions and authenticate the interpretations. Several of the first hermits who had known Bruno and seen how he lived were still alive, too. It would be good to take advantage of their presence and their memories. Undertaking the task now would offer the best guarantee that it would conform to Bruno's plan.

After hesitating for a long time, Guigo began his work,

but he did not make laws. Rather, he codified the life as it was lived at Chartreuse, under the title "The Customs of Our House". He did not impose his personal ideas, but he passed on a tradition, something like those brothers that the prior of Chartreuse occasionally sent to new hermitages to form candidates according to the spirit of Chartreuse. His work was not like a Rule but, more modestly, a *Custumal* (*Customs* or *Consuetudines*). He drew it up in the form of a letter addressed only to the priors who had asked for it. Aware of his responsibilities, however, he put his composition on solid foundations, establishing it firmly upon Bruno's work. He connected it to the epistles of Saint Jerome,[1] the Rule of Saint Benedict, and "other writings whose authority is beyond question".

So, he courageously began what he knew had to be a lengthy and thorny task. To it he brought his own learning, his broad culture, his creative literary talent, his fidelity to Bruno as well as his admiration for him, and his love of solitude and the contemplative life. The completion of the *Customs* took six years, until about 1127. Then Guigo handed over to his brothers at Chartreuse, Portes, Saint-Sulpice, and Meyriat a Code for the eremitical life, which the Carthusian Order still follows. But that will not be treated in this book.[2]

Guigo's work is of great help in trying to reach a better understanding of Bruno's soul and the grace he had received.

[1] Guigo is the author of a critical edition of the Letters of Saint Jerome.

[2] It is not for lack of desire or admiration for Guigo. His *Customs* could be called a "hymn to the contemplative life in solitude". To understand the extent to which the spirit of Bruno and the spirit of Guigo agreed, it is necessary to read some of his chapters, such as those that deal with the appointment of the prior (15), the poor and almsgiving (20), novices (22), the care of the sick (38), why the number of hermits is so small (79), and especially the last chapter, "In Praise of the Solitary Life".

Though his lines are bland, even austere, some of them are packed with meaning and reflect Bruno's human and spiritual riches, which have already been mentioned or at least alluded to. But Guigo's lines are not the result of his abstract reflection. There is abundant documentation for them, because they are a record of forty years of the experience of a group of people, six of whom were inspired and sustained by the physical presence of Bruno. Bruno knew how to give his sons enthusiasm. More than founder of the hermitage of Chartreuse and the Carthusian Order, he was the inspiration for a life of pure contemplation. That is what Pius XI meant in the constitution *Umbratilem*: "In his infinite goodness, which never ceases to provide for the needs and interests of his Church, God chose Bruno, a man of outstanding holiness, to restore the original purity of contemplative life."

In closing, what—according to Bruno and Guigo—would a sketch of "the original purity of contemplative life" look like? A sketch only, because there can be no description. Contemplation is and always remains a paradox for an unspiritual person. The phrase "the monastic mystery" is an accurate statement of the whole contemplative vocation. An even more mysterious mystery is the eremitical mystery: that is, the vocation to live the contemplative life in the solitude and silence of a cell. Despite the profound difference in temperament between the two men, the history of Guigo as revealed in his *Thoughts* and his *Customs* is in accord with the history of Bruno and his writings, and that makes it possible to lift at least a corner of the veil that hides this "eremitical mystery".

A word used by Bruno and Guigo both describes this mystery. The word is *Quies*, and the usual translation of this word is "rest", but that does not clearly convey the divine dimension and the richness of *Quies*. The "quiet" of the Carthusian and faithfulness in exterior practices go together. The word designates the experience of the spiritual abundance of the Christian who even now is founded upon God, "dwells in God", in the words of Saint John, through the events and circumstances of his life—for the Carthusian, through obedience and monastic practices. A verse from Lamentations (3:28), on which Guigo liked to comment, signifies by contrasting words[3] that the contemplative is related to the circumstances of earth as well as the supernatural life: Sedebit *solitarius et tacebit, et* levabit *se supra se* (The solitary will sit and be silent, and he will rise above himself). "Quiet" actually includes everything contained in our word *rest (sedebit)*, that is, calm, peace, silence, orderly thinking, mastery of the heart's passions, etc. But it contains infinitely much more, because it is the hidden movement of the Holy Spirit in the soul: it is a condition of the spirit together with a gift of grace. The soul strives, prepares, and merits it, but it is conferred by God alone. Quiet comes to the soul only from love that totally, even exclusively, desires the living God, the "Father, source and origin of all Divinity, of whom the Son is born and the Holy Spirit proceeds."[4] It comes from that love that is founded upon radical faith in the word and in the salvation of Jesus Christ. Guigo calls one who has this quiet a "quiet Christ",

[3] There is a difficulty here, which everyone who cites texts from the Bible in their ancient form knows very well. Increasing knowledge of the Hebrew language brings out the original meaning of these texts. Today that verse from Lamentations is no longer translated "he will sit in silence and will rise above himself" but "let him sit alone and in silence, for the Lord has laid [the yoke] on him". Guigo's understanding of the verse is kept here, following the Fathers of the Church. It is not used as an authoritative argument any more, but it is a very good way to express a mystical reality.

[4] Bruno's profession of faith. Cf. *Lettres des premiers Chartreux*, I., p. 93.

meaning that something of the joy and peace of the risen Christ dwells in him and radiates from him ("and he will rise above himself"). With Christ he comes to that "freedom of the children of God" of which Saint Paul speaks. He comes to it already and yet never ceases to approach it, because God's presence in him invites him to solitude and silence ("he will sit and be silent"), and in return the silence and solitude assist his progress toward intimacy with God.

If this analysis is correct, the quiet clarifies a great principle of Bruno's and Guigo's spirituality: that is, spiritual virginity. The soul is virgin if it is so strongly attached to God that it is detached from everything that is not God. In contrast, the one without faith, the idolater, whom the Bible vividly calls "prostitute", is attached to anything apart from God. Here it is important not to lose the sense of this asceticism. It doesn't say that the first stage is to detach oneself from the world and then attach oneself to God. It says to prefer God and, in this one act of preferring, to "go in search of the good that is everlasting" and turn away from the things of earth, which are "fleeting shadows". This is the act of the Holy Spirit, who was the source of Bruno's vocation. In the little garden at Adam's house, Bruno, Raoul le Verd, and Fulco le Borgne were filled "with fervent love for God", and from that love sprang their basic resolution, which became their vow "to leave the fleeting shadows of the world to go in search of the good that is eternal". Was this an exceptional grace? In the degree that Bruno experienced it, certainly it was. But it can also be said to be the fundamental option that all Christians must make on the day they decide to live the fullness of their baptism. Guigo wrote, "It is with good reason that the human soul is troubled as long as it is: that is, as long as it loves something besides God."[5] God does not accept a divided heart. Each one, in his own way and according to his own vocation, will meet this requirement of detachment and attachment, but the requirement itself is not negotiable. It is inescapable. No Christian, nor any "human soul", can avoid it.

Optimam partem. Bruno and Guigo present this quiet as the "better part" that Mary chose, a few days before Jesus' Passion [cf. John 12:1], when he stopped at the house of Lazarus in Bethany. The contrast between Mary's contemplation and Martha's activity is a traditional theme among the Fathers of the Church. Guigo takes it up in the *Customs*, but he gives it a new meaning and a new emotion. In the very words of the Lord he claims for Carthusians the right to live a contemplative life in solitude, like Mary at the feet of Jesus, which—though at some distance—includes the legitimate and holy activities of Martha, such as hospitality, almsgiving, and service. "Mary has chosen the better part and it shall not be taken from her." When he says "the better", the Lord was not only praising it but also placing it above the laborious activity of her sister. Saying "it shall not be taken from her", he defended it and exempted it from involvement in the troubles and anxieties of Martha, legitimate though they were.[6] Is this to flee from the labors, anguish, and sadness of the world? No. The emphasis is on profound faith. Like Bruno, Guigo thinks that for the spiritual health and apostolic effectiveness of the Church it is necessary that

[5] Pensée no. 399.

[6] This commentary of Guigo on the words "it shall not be taken away" deserves to be underlined. The Latin and even the Greek Fathers had given an eschatological meaning to this promise. They said it was in the future that this better part will not be taken from Mary. Guigo is the only one to give it this emphatic meaning for the present. This very day Mary can and should keep to the better part, that is, the contemplation of the Savior.

some souls be free for the pure contemplative life "in the weak measure that it is possible in this world, as in a mirror and darkly". Mary prays both for herself and for those who are vowed, like Martha, to other works. And so it is for those whose vocation is to combine Martha and Mary in their lives: Martha's work is made effective by Mary's prayer.

This study of Carthusian quiet should conclude with a comment on two traits that strongly mark the character of Bruno and of Guigo: balance and simplicity. *Quiet* and *balance* are almost synonyms. But the purity, the beauty, the grandeur of the contemplative ideal, as Bruno lived it and proposed it, could make one think—and fear—that this balance is of a superior and exceptional kind. Certainly the Carthusian vocation is a rare one of a new kind. A clear call from God is necessary. But that does not mean this ideal is reserved for extraordinary souls. Carthusian balance does not require exceptional gifts of nature or of grace. What it requires is simplicity, simplicity of heart, the simplicity of the "little ones", the humble people of the Gospel; the simplicity that comes from integrity and faith, from detachment and hope, from guilelessness and love; the simplicity that radiates from the letter of Bruno to the brethren at Chartreuse and that Guigo requires in all the observances of his *Customs*.

In choosing solitude, silence, and separation from the world, Bruno paradoxically came to understand the heart of all humanity. For him and for the education of all, the basic desire that motivates everyone here below was enough: the desire to escape from all that is fleeting and be united with what is still, fixed, eternal: *Fugitiva relinquere . . . captare æterna.* His two companions, Raoul le Verd and Fulco le Borgne, knew the same desire as Bruno on that day. Bruno alone pursued it, and he alone knew the fullness of joy. "Only those who have experienced the solitude and silence of the wilderness can know what benefit and divine joy they bring to those who love them." Carthusian quiet cannot be described perfectly. It is a mystery that can be understood only by those who have experienced it, by "those who love it".

~

"Like a syllable in a poem," said Guigo in one of his Thoughts,[7] "as the world goes round everything receives its proper share of space and time." Who would presume to determine Bruno's "proper share of space and time" in the poem of the redemption? Aren't these among the ones whose spiritual experience transcends space and time, whom the Father places with his Son, Jesus Christ, at the still and eternal center of the world's history? *Stat crux dum volvitur orbis*.

[7] Pensée no. 181.

Index of Persons

Lightning Source UK Ltd.
Milton Keynes UK
UKOW04f1425281017
311777UK00001B/11/P

9 780852 449240